D1145232

TALLER TODAY

BY THE SAME AUTHOR

Short Fiction
Bars of America

Novels
Double Helix Fall
Putting Out
English Weather

NEIL FERGUSON

TALLER TODAY

Fragments of Childhood

TELEGRAM

First published 2013 by Telegram

1

ISBN 978 1 84659 151 8
eISBN 978 1 84659 153 2

A full cip record for this book is available from the British Library.

Printed and bound by Bookwell in Finland

TELEGRAM
26 Westbourne Grove, London W2 5RH
www.telegrambooks.com

For Sarah, Kate, Max

Home

In the winter of 1953 I lived with my father in a mews garage in Bayswater. By the time I arrived most of the garage machinery had been removed and a few domestic comforts installed: a pair of old leather armchairs, a couple of Aladdin paraffin heaters, some worn-out Persian carpets, a standard lamp, a kitchen table, odd pots and pans, a teapot. In addition to these bare necessities the garage was well stocked with interesting mechanical and electrical appliances Dad had picked up second-hand in Portobello Road: a mains gramophone with speaker, an office typewriter, a toaster, several wireless sets, some functioning, most awaiting repair. Still suspended from the ceiling were the chains of the engine hoist; boards and carpet had been laid over the concrete floor and the inspection pit. A niff of engine oil combined with the aroma of Sobranie pipe tobacco, Senior Service cigarettes and paraffin gave the place its own delicious smell. Dad had a room in the back with a big bed, and a cubbyhole where he had his drawing board. I had a cot in an alcove under the blocked-off stairs, although I nearly always slept in Dad's bed. The entrance to the garage was through a wooden roller shutter that was never raised throughout the time I lived there. It contained a wicket door, opened with a Yale key, that was just large enough for a person to step through. In January Dad had stepped through it carrying me wrapped in a blanket, half asleep, from the back seat of his car, which he had just navigated through a thick fog, an old-fashioned London pea-souper that tried to follow us in like a cat.

I didn't know why my mother wasn't with us. I knew I had a brother and a sister, because I had met them occasionally. We would probably run into each other sooner or later, like cousins several times removed. The arrangement didn't strike me as particularly unusual. As we moved from one sort of rented accommodation to another in pursuit of Dad's work, we children sometimes found ourselves parked in different places for indeterminate periods. Whether or not this nomadic life was agreeable to our mother, it suited our dad, to whom the notion of settling down was anathema. He had never hankered after his own bricks and mortar nor any of the other requisites of a settled life that my mum hankered after. On the contrary, he only felt comfortable when his circumstances were provisional, his commitments ones he could easily get out of: the contract that would come to an end, the converted mews garage a man in a pub had allowed him to rent for practically nothing on condition he vacated it when the man found a developer to sell it to. Dad refused at all costs to be tied down.

The mews bisected the obtuse angle of Westbourne Terrace where it ran into Bayswater Road, across the road from Kensington Gardens and round the corner from Lancaster Gate Underground station. This partly bombed six-storey block of imposing, once splendid, now forlorn Victorian terraced residences, of genteel old maids' parlours cheek by jowl with tarts' bedsits, was sold off in a job lot shortly after we lived there in order for it to be knocked down and redeveloped. A twenty-storey matchbox-shaped hotel was built on the site of the elegant crumbling terraces where these events in my childhood took place, a concrete reminder – to a later version of myself when he passed on the top deck of a 12 or 88 bus – of the process by which, in due course, one era in a person's life is replaced by another.

During the day Dad worked at the drawing board in his cubbyhole in his overcoat and muffler, spectacles resting on his bald crown, sky-blue Staedtler pencil behind his ear, slide-rule at hand, drawing pen inking along the bevelled edge of the T-square, cigarette burning the ledge of the board. On the shelf next to his board: empty tea-stained cups, his massive books of logarithms, bottles of Swan ink, sharpened pencils and single-sided razor blades with which to resharpen them, ink-swabbed handkerchiefs, his teeth. Around him: impregnable silence.

While Dad worked I kept out of his way, playing in the asbestos-block bunker he had built for me at the front of the garage, machine-gunning the occasional passer-by. I had the run of the mews which, because it was a dead-end, was free of traffic. Or else, under the guidance of my friends Alf and his wife Dot, who had a flower and fruit stall outside the Tube station, I crossed at the traffic lights to the Kensington Gardens side of Bayswater Road. I explored the park, patrolling the drained fountains under the gaze of Edward Jenner (1749–1823), waiting to ambush, armed to the teeth, some invisible pursuer, until my stomach told me it was time for me to return home for my tea and then Alf or Dot saw me back across the road.

Dad prepared our tea in a hay-box. Because there was no gas in the garage, he had rigged up a Smiths Crisps tin in which he had placed, in the hay, the element from an electric iron. The meals he cooked in the hay-box were exciting and unpredictable, like schoolboy experiments carried out while the science master is out of the room. Later he got hold of a Baby Belling and on this he boiled water in a saucepan for tea. With our tea we ate brown-sugar sandwiches, warmed-up tinned mince and, now and then, a round sausage that Dad addressed as Chief Among the Pudding Race. For breakfast we ate porridge that had simmered all night in the hay-box so that it cooked to such a fine consistency you could cut it with a knife and on which Dad wrote my name with Golden Syrup.

After a couple more hours at the drawing board, Dad shaved in the big rectangular sink – once a week my bath – and put on a shirt and tie and left for the pub, the Victoria and Albert, which was conveniently close by, two doors down from the garage, on the corner of Westbourne Terrace and Bayswater Road. He put me down with my golliwog and my car in his bed under his old Navy greatcoat and, if I was still awake when he left, he turned the radio on, tuned to the Light Programme, quietly playing dance music. In the darkness the perforated top of the cylindrical iron paraffin heater threw an illuminated pattern onto the ceiling, which I found enchanting.

I didn't particularly miss my mother, nor my brother and sister. I was happy to live with my dad, who had a wonderful collection of pencils, India rubbers, emery boards, stencils and scraps of paper; who let me roam unsupervised in the park with my spear and bow and arrows, innocent of the dangers that older siblings would have been only too happy to frighten me to death with. It was January, February, March – first cold, then stormy, then cold again. I wore the navy-blue wool mittens and balaclava my mum had knitted and sent to me from wherever she was, and over the balaclava a peaked leatherette cap with a strap under the chin like an RAF flying helmet. I had a silk scarf of my dad's tucked into a windjammer. My hot breath steamed in the cold air like smoke from one of the departing engines in Paddington station, whose *shsh-shsh-shsh* I imitated, my arms slowly rotating like piston-cranks. My wellington boots, scrunching the frost, left their shape in the white grass. With my clutch of weapons I was surely the fearsomest-looking five-year-old ever to stalk this neck of the woods.

Except for the rare arm-in-arm couple, a soldier and his girl, or uniformed nurse pushing a perambulator, and the distant sheep grazing on the far side of the Serpentine, Kensington Gardens was deserted, silent, bleak. It was a blank landscape waiting to be transformed by a child's imagination into the domain of the lone hunter, of the hunted airman, baled out over enemy territory. In the absence of grown-ups to measure myself against, I wasn't small; I was just the right size. My only fears were those I deliberately conjured up to frighten myself with. From the Italian fountains as far as the sooty stone arbour facing the Long Water I roamed the timbered plains where lone rooks cruised overhead like spotter aircraft and harmless-looking civilians in belted raincoats, walking dogs, were to be watched in case they turned upon the unwary. Wary, I skulked in the undergrowth along the water's edge with my catapult loaded, stalked by an unseen, pitiless enemy, occasionally disguising myself as a child and lobbing crusts in the direction of mute swans. Birds abounded – squadrons of mallard, convoys of moorhen, the deadly supermarine cormorant, a lone heron banking slowly like a Dornier 17 approaching its designated target. I lurked in the undergrowth and bushes, picking up things of interest: scarlet berries, the carcasses of insects and birds, the fag-ends of conversations couples dropped as they passed close to where I was hidden, under the impression that they were alone.

At the furthest point of my wanderings, where the rim of my known world edged into *terra incognita*, I had a secret place in which to conceal myself and favoured objects. On the sloping west bank, between the Long Water and Queen Caroline's Temple (1734), a squat half-dead oak tree had an aperture in its trunk just large enough for a small person to squeeze through into its hollow centre, hide his car, store his weapons, read his comics and eat custard cream biscuits out of the wind. There, in the great game of *Had* that I played with the Invisible Forces of Darkness, I was safe from betrayal and capture. I was *Home*.

My Car

My car was a brand-new racing green MG two-seat roadster with chrome wire wheels and collapsible roof that Dad had taken a shine to in a shop window in Knightsbridge. He had marched into the shop and written a cheque for it on the spot – in much the same way he bought cars for himself. In all his affairs Dad favoured the impulsive extravagant gesture over decisions based upon deliberation and prudence. Especially when it came to buying motor cars.

Dad was interested in all manner of machines, engines, motors and gizmos, electrical or mechanical, but it was motor cars he loved best. He loved owning them, driving them, mending them, talking about them, and he spent all his money on them. He understood how they worked and why they went wrong. He basked in the glory their luxury reflected, because a fine suit, a military bearing and a beautiful motor car would always guarantee that a chap's cheque would be accepted. As a young man he had owned, among other marks, a bull-nosed Morris, a racing green 4½-litre Bentley and, in 1924, a mustard-coloured six-cylinder Minerva roadster, which was the reason, he claimed, he now had to work for a living. The Minerva had been the big love of his life, an old flame he recalled with great fondness. Whenever he talked about his past, places he had visited, women he had lived with or the adventures he had had, his reminiscence was accompanied by a wistful account of the motor car he had owned at the time, the marque and model, engine size, even registration number: *Foxie and I were driving through France in the Minerva on our way to Monte . . .* All cars played up eventually and involved an element of heartache, but they were without the guile, the wilfulness, the volatility and the treachery of people. They didn't answer back.

I was thrilled to bits with my MG. Larger and more exquisitely detailed than a Corgi or Dinky model, with a pressed metal body, removable moulded rubber tyres, including a spare in the boot, genuine suspension and doors that opened and closed, my car was lovely beyond words and it accompanied me everywhere. I raced it – *her*, Dad would have me say – around the rim of the drained fountains in the park. The sloped surface of these stone basins was ideal for observing the car performing at speed over a convincingly hair-raising Silverstone terrain. At night I garaged my car in the crook of my elbow, alongside the golly my mum had knitted for me.

Occasionally I left my most treasured possession concealed under dead leaves in the secret place in the hollow oak tree in Kensington Gardens. I abandoned it for short, increasingly less short periods, returning – my heart thumping with fear – to find out if it was where I had left it. I did this as an act of bravado and to test the secrecy of the place, to assay my powers against those of the Invisible Forces of Darkness, whom I knew lurked in every shadow. It was foolish of me. I came to understand soon enough that I should never have brought my insignificant person to Their attention.

Dad's own car at this period was a clotted cream-coloured Riley saloon that had a reassuring growl when he put his foot down, with a graceful outline not dissimilar to my sporty MG, front wings that swept back from chrome headlamps to a short running board, soft cerise leather upholstery and a polished walnut dash that included an HMV radio. I liked to climb into the front seat of the Riley, conveniently parked outside the garage gate, and curl up under a blanket with my golly in the leather upholstery while rain drummed onto the roof of the car. If Dad had left the key in the ignition, I pushed the Home Service preset button of the HMV to hear *Children's Hour* or *Paul Temple, Private Detective.* All I understood of the adult programmes were the catch phrases, which were meaningless; of *Paul Temple* the sound of gunshots, the screech of car tyres and the signature tune, which I hummed while I acted out my adventures. We had nothing as comfy in the garage and so Dad's car served as an armchair and sitting room.

On those occasions Dad needed to drive somewhere and he couldn't leave me alone, he took me with him. It was a treat to sit in the front seat of the Riley – which Dad sometimes referred to as Old Mother Riley – as he drove her out of Paddington to visit friends. The engine roared when he put his foot down on the stretch of open road between Kensington Gardens and Hyde Park from Victoria Gate to Alexandra Gate. One of these friends was a beautiful French woman called Titine, a painter who lived on a houseboat moored in the Thames on Chelsea Reach. While Dad and Titine and their friends smoked and drank and talked, I drew pictures with Titine's coloured pencils until I fell asleep in her berth – the boat rocking gently as its weight shifted on the tide – and it was time for Dad to carry me up the gangplank onto terra firma and drive us home.

Although my MG was my only toy, not counting my golliwog, I didn't feel the want of any other. Dad was skilled at knocking out weapons – bows and arrows, spears, daggers, catapults, swords. He had a knack for that sort of thing. The twenty minutes he spent fashioning them for me kept me from under his feet all day. With my arsenal of weapons and my car I was content and complete, without longings for things to be different, because I couldn't conceive how they could be different, either better or worse. I accepted my life in a converted garage, my dad with his beautiful motor car, me with mine.

Later, when the Invisible Forces of Darkness eventually noticed my existence and accepted my puny challenge and, cornered, I was forced to turn and face a malign fate alone, it was only this talisman, my beloved MG roadster my dad had bought me, that stood between me and annihilation.

The Storm

The first day of February. Overnight, the weather had turned wet and windy, quite stormy, in fact. In the morning slate roof tiles, chimney pots and other debris from the surrounding buildings lay shattered on the cobbles outside the garage. Tin dustbins on their sides were bouncing along like footballs, their contents distributed in every direction. It was a marvellous sight. Dad, carrying me under his arm like a parcel the two doors down to the V&A for a spot of lunch, had to keep tight hold of me – as I had to keep hold of my car – to prevent me from being blown away.

The V&A had only two small bars, a Public for workmen in overalls and a cosy private den with a carpet and a coal fire for my dad and his friends. At lunchtime these were the only people in the Private Bar and I was passed around and fussed over by the women, who were fragrant with gardenia perfume and cigarette smoke. I was kissed with their waxy red lips, sat on their laps, let go in case I scuffed their skirts, forgotten about and eventually ignored. I wandered between steaming flannel trousers and deliciously silky stockings – or sat on the floor with my meat paste sandwich, vrooming my car in front of the coal fire while Dad and his cronies discussed the weather and the pictures in the newspapers of the *Princess Victoria*, the ferry from Stranraer to Belfast that had capsized and sunk in the night with a hundred passengers lost. Dad, as the recognised authority on naval matters, gave his opinion that the bloody fools must have left the bow doors open for her to have gone down as quickly as she did. He tended to get worked up about drownings at sea. As Captain Hook feared the Crocodile, Dad had a horror of open water, being such an indifferent swimmer, and he didn't go near the wet stuff if he could help it, as if he had some premonition that it was his destiny to end up in it. By tradition, he told me, sailors were not encouraged to learn to swim in the Royal Navy, on the humanitarian grounds that, in the event of their falling overboard, they would drown more quickly.

I had been aware that my dad was a Navy man for almost as long as I had known he was my dad. The fact inhabited his every utterance, his manner and his taste. He spoke like a naval officer, dressed like one, smoked like one, swore like one. His medals were in a cardboard box in a drawer: two for the Great War, five for Second World War and the orange and black ribbon of his Tsarist decoration, the Order of St Catherine (Third Class).

His Navy sword hung in its scabbard from a nail in the garage. Alone, I had lifted it from the hook on the wall, unsheathed the blade and swashed the invisible bucklers of invisible pirates.

We had a framed photograph of him in the dress uniform of a midshipman, wearing his sword, on his passing out of the Royal Naval College at Dartmouth, dated 1918.

So it was a puzzle to learn – much later – that he had been demobbed after the Second World War as a leading seaman. I did know, though, that he had had all his teeth pulled as a consequence of his decision to go to sea. I often watched him take his false uppers and lowers from the ledge on the drawing board where he kept them and put them into his mouth before he set foot out of the garage. The upper set had a cigarette burn across the palate.

'Did they pull them *all* out?' I asked him.

'Every bloody one of them! It hurt like buggery!'

'Why did they do that?'

'They were rotten – too many sweeties – and there's no dentist on a man-o'-war, my boy. Just a chief stoker who pulls teeth a shilling each, the only anaesthetic a tot of rum. Last place you want to get toothache is on shipboard. A sailor can't do his job with sore teeth.'

Living with Dad was like serving on board one of Her Majesty's capital ships. He was captain – that went without saying – and I was a member of the crew, anyone from first mate to cabin boy. He addressed me as a captain would one of his men, now intimately as a comrade-at-arms, now barking an order to a rating, according to what he considered my rank to be at that particular moment. Although he could get shirty when he wanted to, and I could get as shirty as he could, by and large we were a happy ship. He wasn't quite Captain Bligh and I was no Fletcher Christian. When things went well, it was splice the main brace: rum and hornpipes, double rations of Golden Syrup on the porridge. When things went wrong, as they did do from time to time, he swore violently, sometimes in French. If I happened to be nearby at such a moment he might, for the benefit of my education, declaim the names of Nelson's battles in chronological order: *Copenhagen! Ushant! Nile and Trafalgar!*

The dirty weather, as Dad called it, didn't go away. At times it was a steady downpour, followed by salvos of lightning and thunder which, Dad explained, was the sound of negative static electricity searching for a positive pole into which to earth itself. At other times a noisy, blustery wind blew between 6 (strong breeze) and 8 (gale) on the Beaufort scale. I was forced to spend a lot of time indoors, keeping myself amused because even my dad could see that it wasn't weather a small boy should be out in. I sat on the carpet next to the paraffin stove, cutting out and colouring in the photographs in Dad's copy of the *Manchester Guardian*: our beautiful, new, and as yet uncrowned queen and her pretty sister; houses under water up to the windows; men in dressing-gowns and flat caps rowing past shops. When he wasn't leaning over his drawing board, Dad, who was sensitive to national disaster, paced the floor and smoked his pipe, as if he were waiting for a telegram from the prime minister seeking his advice about what should be done.

In the normal course of things Dad and I got on best when we weren't in each other's way. If he could ever be said to have had a philosophy of child-rearing it was that children should not be heard and not seen either. The advantage to me of this policy was that I was free to go about my own business, no questions asked. If I was at a loose end I had to find something to do, to loll in Old Mother Riley or play in Kensington Gardens. During this period, however, with the storms in London and the flooding throughout the country, the sense of crisis outside the garage made us more tolerant of each other. Dad played draughts with me on his chessboard with ha'pennies, my heads against his tails. After we had played draughts, over a plate of brown sugar sandwiches he told me stories about his life. Dad liked to tell stories, especially stories in which he was the protagonist, almost as much as he liked to drive motor cars. These stories – which, if I happened to be the only audience on hand, he told to me – took place *Before the War* or *During the War*, although I had no way of knowing then which war he was referring to.

'Mother had taken a house for August in Greystones, a pretty little village in County Wicklow, just south of Bray. It was another big ugly building but in a lovely part of Ireland. The hills rolled right down to the sand dunes into the sea. All of

Ireland was part of the British Empire then, don't forget. We had crossed the Irish Sea but it wasn't as if we had gone abroad. The King's writ still ran south of Armagh.

'Earlier that year the Seine had flooded and Paris had been under water, which is how I can date the episode exactly: 1910. I would have been – what? – seven. Duncan fourteen, Ian twelve. People still talked about how the President of the Republic had had to be rowed to the Assembly. On the marvellous beach there we children built Paris in the sand with the Seine, the Île de Paris, the Eiffel Tower, out of sand, sticks and bits of flotsam – so that the city would flood when the tide came in at the end of the day, floating our little paper boat for the President of the Republic.

'My brothers, Duncan and Ian, always included me in their games and projects. They never pulled rank. Since our Dada had died when I was a babe in arms, the boys, as the two men in the house, shouldered their responsibility. The girls, Margaret and Mary, tended to fret about me getting sand in my knickers. I was piggy in the middle. It's bloody awful being the youngest in a family, as you'll find out for yourself soon enough.

'It was a marvellous holiday, one of the last we all had together. The local people couldn't have been kinder, especially towards us children. God knows, they had no reason to be kind to these little English so-and-so's with their airs, their servants and Army and Navy Stores kit, but they were. I spent many happy hours roaming the hills pursuing butterflies with my net in the company of a young local boy my own age. Fritillaries, skippers, blues, yellows, the occasional monarch that had blown across the Atlantic. There were many more butterflies then than there are now. Mother presided over picnic tea on the beach like the old Queen Empress at her Durbar in India. We ate potted meat sandwiches and drank ginger beer or tea on our square tartan rug, ignorant of the gale-force turbulence that was about to strike our little island. This – we didn't know it at the time – was the calm before the storm.

'In the evening the mackerel used to come close inshore. You could wade out and catch them with shrimping nets, they came in so close. On the sand, Duncan and Ian built a fire out of driftwood and we sat around it and ate the fish with our fingers as the sun set behind us. In the fading light, Duncan told us ghost stories . . .'

Dad unwound his yarns until, entangled in their incomprehensible beauty, I fell asleep – and then he put me to bed.

'The next occasion I visited Ireland, it was a foreign country . . .'

On Sunday morning, during a lull in the bad weather, we wrapped up – Dad in his Navy greatcoat, I in my windjammer, mittens and leatherette helmet – and headed across Bayswater Road into the teeth of the wind. Kensington Gardens resembled the aftermath of a battle zone. Trees lay horizontal. Clouds roiled and the wind buffeted you in perplexing, thrilling gusts, whipping the grass, which was strewn with branches, pieces of bark, bits of storm debris. Massive trunks had snapped in two like pencils. These were exciting to clamber onto, then, bestriding the colossus, to walk the length of the trunk. The excitement was made more intense by the feeling that I was present at an extraordinary event, something even grown-ups marvelled at: such massive living things laid so low. Others besides ourselves had braved the remnants of the storm to inspect the damage for themselves. Gentlemen in smart overcoats with their ladies in fox furs and their obedient dogs stood about, pointing with their rolled umbrellas, commenting to each other. At the Round Pond the men who had brought scale model sailing ships on pram chassis to race across it stood about in glum clumps with their hands in their pockets, looking up at the sky and down at the choppy surface of the water, murmuring to each other while shaking their heads. It was a disappointment not to see any full-sheeted clippers beating before the wind, no close-hauled yachts luffing into it at a perilous angle.

Dad, who always kept a weather eye open for a congenial-looking face to button-hole – the negative static electricity inside him searching for a positive pole into which to earth itself – fell into conversation with a chap in a bow-tie, out walking with his wife and four children – a pretty girl of about my own age, a couple of boys and a baby in a pram I didn't bother to look at. They let me play with their dog, Jack. Jack was everything you could have wanted a dog to be: a well-bred Cairn terrier with a sense of humour. I thought the whole family enchanting. A father and a mother, four children dressed in sensible clothes, and a dog, they challenged my idea of what a family was supposed to look like, calling to each other in clear, confident voices.

While the two dads sounded each other out, we children played Had with Jack. Released from the garage into the open air, chasing and being chased by other children, I was delighted. I had never known what it was to have friends, let alone a dog, and this happy cameo stayed with me throughout my childhood. It became my yardstick for what family life should be like. One day I would belong to one of these.

Without warning, at the whim of the adults and before we had finished our game, it was time – nearly opening time, in other words – to go our separate ways. I said goodbye to Jack as Dad strode off in the direction of Knightsbridge. I had to trot to keep up with him. It would never have occurred to him to slow down on my account.

'Interesting young fellow,' Dad remarked to the invisible adult striding alongside him. 'Ex-captain in army intelligence, if that isn't a contradiction in terms . . .'

We walked as far as the bridge over the Serpentine and there we paused because I was beginning to tire. At the dead centre of the bridge, he lifted me up and laid me flat upon the stone balustrade so that I could lean over the edge and look down onto the water. He wanted me to see the wind churning it into a fine spray, droplets of which wet my face. If he hadn't held me tight I should have been blown over. I felt safe enough in his arms but also exhilaratingly terrified by the furious scene below: green water chopping and crashing against the sheer load-bearing stone verticals of the bridge. It didn't occur to me for a moment that he would drop me in it.

'. . . About this time of year in 1943 I was on HMS *Osprey*, which was a rather lovely Type 22 frigate. We were in the North Sea, on escort duty for Convoy PQ16, up into the Barents Sea, en route for Murmansk.

'In the morning of 17 February I happened to be on the bridge along with the commander, who had been there all night. I had just begun my trick on deck after two hours lying to on my bunk in my sea boots, so it must have been soon after eight o'clock. It was bloody awful weather. Waves twenty, thirty feet high. In the half-light everything was the colour of snot – the sea, the sky, the forward deck – and the old girl was rolling and pitching like a bloody seesaw. Water was pouring over the bows and gunwales. Freezing spindrift was in your hair and your eyes, down your neck. Your eyebrows and eyelashes froze. Your hand became welded to any piece of metal you were foolish enough to place it against for more than a moment. It was maddening.

'We knew from the Admiralty that there was a U-boat out there. At least one. A whole bloody pack of the blighters, for all we knew. And if the enemy *was* out there, with dawn just breaking, he would see us silhouetted against it long before we saw him, peeping out from the depths of the darkness. Every man was standing to, at action stations. Our nerves were raw – we were all peering into the murk, praying to God we wouldn't see anything – when there was an almighty bloody explosion. A ship about thirty degrees on our port side had been hit. Turned out it was the *Isis*, an old New York grain-carrier. She went up like a Roman candle and suddenly you could see every bloody ship in the convoy, clear as a Sunday morning at Cowes.

'The Old Man asked for full steam. No point hanging about at the snail's pace of the rest of the convoy. We had to skedaddle. By the time we came abreast of the *Isis* – we were the nearest of her escort ships – she was already arsy-versy. Her stern was almost over her bows and she was going down fast. Frankly, you just wished she'd hurry up about it. But it wasn't a pleasant sight. By the light of the fire on her you could see men jumping into the water and swimming away from their ship. Even over that storm-force wind you could hear them in the water, calling out to us, their comrades, to come to their aid, but we couldn't haul to and pick them up. That was out of the question. We just held to our course at full speed, which was twenty-two knots. No one blamed the Old Man. He was following standing orders. If we had stopped engines we would have made ourselves a sitting duck for the U-boat that was probably watching us, waiting to see what we would do.

You daren't risk a capital ship like that. We were at war. We left the poor blighters to their fate. As cold-blooded as that.

'It's a pitiful sound, the crying of men in the water, especially when they are men you're supposed to be protecting, leaving them to drown in the freezing sea. It didn't matter that they were boys from Milwaukee, Kansas, North Dakota, Iowa. That only made it worse. We hadn't just let ourselves down, we had let our friends down too. With heavy hearts we watched her go under. It only took about five minutes for the sea to douse her glim.

'We lost two more ships before forenoon watch and all we, their escorts, had done was to scarper without firing a shot. Left a nasty taste in the mouth, I can tell you . . .'

The Gang

From time to time Dad's friends – *the Gang*, he called them – came back with him after closing time in the pub. I was delighted whenever this happened, when the door to the garage opened and one by one, sh-shing and pushing each other, giggling, they stepped through the gate into my dreams. There was no proper door to the room at the back where Dad and I slept, just a curtain slung between two nails, so I was able to hear everything – the clink of glasses, the gramophone switched on – and through the crack in the curtain catch glimpses of what the Gang was up to. One or two couples danced. The women kept their fur coats on when they danced because even with both paraffin heaters burning the garage was chilly. Those who didn't dance talked, exchanged jokes and stories, laughed – all at the same time, it sounded like. And drank: the men Scotch, the ladies Booth's Gin with Angostura bitters. Having just spent several hours in the pub, they were pretty tanked up already.

I was careful not to wake completely nor get out of bed. If I did that I knew what would happen: I would have my leg pulled by the men, be embraced by the ladies and, engulfed in their unfamiliar fug, be allowed to pour two fingers of gin and shake the bitters into it before being bundled back to bed. I preferred to listen to them from the security of the dark, unseen, snug under the blankets and Dad's Navy greatcoat.

If one of the party succeeded in operating the mains-powered gramophone, she would trawl through his collection of jumble-sale 78 rpm records: Al Bowlly, Geraldo and his Savoy Hotel Orchestra, 'Whispering' Jack Smith, Jean Sablon, who sang in French, Leslie 'Hutch' Hutchinson, who was coloured, 'Snakehips' Johnston, killed on stage when the Café de Paris took a direct hit. I was familiar with these bandleaders and singers from having played the records myself. It was exciting to be there and not be there, awake when I shouldn't have been, anticipating the next record, drifting in and out of sleep.

Or else they found a station on the radio that played dance music. As well as the gramophone Dad owned several wireless sets he had picked up in the market or in the street. He was unable to pass an electrical appliance that had been thrown out with the rubbish without bringing it home. Opposite his cubbyhole was the original garage workbench and on this were a couple of wireless sets, with or without their casing. Dad was not a great listener to the radio, except the nine o'clock and the six o'clock News, *In Town Tonight* and the *General Shipping Forecast for Inshore Waters*. He had no ear for music and he didn't have time for comedy programmes or dramas. It was the process of radiophonic technology, the movement of electrons in patterns that replicated sound waves, that fascinated him, rather than the content of the emitted signal. His radios performed variably, the valves glowing and dimming – or not glowing at all. He often transferred the valves from one model to another so you only found out which of them was working that day by a process of trial and error.

One night the Gang turned up in force, about a dozen of them. I half-woke and half-recognised who was present from their voices: Begbie, Doreen and Gordon, Zoltan the Hungarian, Jock White, Alexei Duvalier who was Swiss, Violet, whom everyone called Vi, Titine. Others whose names I didn't know. Except for Begbie, I liked the ladies best, who wanted to pick me up and crush me in their embrace as if I was *their* little boy. They were like Mum in some respects, quite different to her in others. Like her they had nice wavy hair, soft bosoms, skin that smelt of flowery soap, but they tended to wear more make-up than Mum did, and powder came off on your skin if it came in too close contact with their face. None of them was as young as my mum, nor as pretty, in my opinion.

The voices rose and fell. The armchairs were pulled back to make a space on the carpet to dance on. The music started up: Ray Noble and the Palais de Dance Orchestra: 'Comin' In On A Wing And A Prayer'. The sound of women laughing, of men bellowing to make themselves heard. Then the curtain to the room where I was lying was pushed aside and two people were in the room with me, one of whom, I could tell from her perfume, was a woman. Standing in the dark against the wall next to the curtain, they didn't speak to each other. They just pressed their bodies together, pulled each other's clothes about the way I had seen couples do in the park when they thought no one was looking. I watched these two, although they couldn't see me in the dark lying under Dad's coat. They thought they were alone. Then they sat on the end of Dad's bed and for a moment I thought they were going to get into it but they didn't. She lay back while he put his hands under her clothes and kissed her face and neck and bosom. He said something I couldn't hear and she whispered *All right* and they stood up. She fastened her blouse and pulled down her skirt and they slipped out of the room while the rest of the Gang was dancing. Fred Astaire was singing 'There may be trouble ahead . . . There may be teardrops to shed . . . Let's face the music and dance . . .'

I was beginning to drift back to sleep amid the laughter of clarinets, the braying of trombones, the tinkling of glasses. Then I heard Dad shouting: *Oh, pipe down, you bloody fool!* This was followed by a crash. A woman screamed. The needle scratched and the music – Dinah Shaw singing 'Baby, It's Cold Outside' – came to an abrupt stop. I was out of bed in a jiffy. I stood behind the curtain, peering out into the bright light.

Two men were scrapping, one of them I could see was a big man, Gordon, one of my favourites. I didn't recognise the other one. Arms were flaying, fists swinging. A woman, the one who had been inside my room, was pulling at the man I didn't know, shouting *Stop it! Stop it!* Then I saw Dad. He was standing between the two men, his arms at right angles to his body as if he were a policeman directing the traffic. Dad was easily as tall as Gordon but without the bulk. Then I heard him cry out, *Ow! My eye!* Then: *You bloody sod! My drawing eye!* Then: *I'll never draw again!*

I ran into the room. Dad was holding his right eye, blood pouring from it. I was frightened. Nobody was laughing now. The sight of blood – of a small boy holding his dad, getting his blood over himself – had sobered everyone up.

'Luke, I'm sorry!'

'Oh bugger off, you oaf!'

One of the women fetched Dad some water and a flannel and bathed his eye. Violet put me on her lap and comforted me. I was crying, afraid that my dad was going to die or at least go blind in his drawing eye. After I had been calmed down my blood-sodden pyjamas were removed and I was put back to bed. The party broke up and the next thing I knew it was morning and Dad was snoring in the bed next to me.

I put on my clothes – the ones I had taken off the night before – and lined up the bottles, smelt the glasses and pretended to puff at the cold dog ends, as was my habit. It was my job to separate out the beer bottles, the ones you got money back from, before Mrs Reardon arrived and threw them out with the ones Dad called *dead marines*. Half-finished glasses, bottles of beer, gin and other drinks were balanced on almost every horizontal surface. Living in such proximity to a pub, there was no shortage of glasses – big ones you needed two hands to lift, littler ones with red lipstick marks on the rims. The ashtrays overflowed with ash and butts. When Mrs Reardon did arrive Dad left me with her while he referred himself to St Mary's Hospital, round the corner in Praed Street, to have his eye looked at. Mrs Reardon cleared the mess up without a word, as she did every Monday and Friday. At least there wasn't a chap asleep on the chairs this morning, stirring out of his hangover, looking for his shoes.

Dad returned from the hospital wearing a green eye-patch. Within half an hour he was back in his cubbyhole, alternately poring over his books of logarithms and leaning over his drawing board, the patch flicked up over his drawing glasses. His eye was fine. He tried to wear his eye-patch but it got on his nerves. In the end, he only bothered with it on his visits to the pub. For a few days he cut a piratical dash in the Victoria and Albert.

Accommodation

I was the one with the eye problem, as it turned out, although it wasn't something that particularly bothered me at the time. I could see perfectly well. Wasn't it me who found Dad's keys or teeth or wallet or cigarette-case or lighter which he had put down and forgotten where? I could throw and catch a ball and read the bus number before Dad could. I was able to peruse the pictures in the *Beano*. Neither of my eyes bothered me. But it was during the period I was living at the garage that my relationship with the ophthalmic profession began. It was one that was going to last, on and off, for the rest of my life.

I had what the optician in Dollond & Aitchison in Notting Hill Gate called a 'lazy eye'. With my right eye I could easily see things far and near. It did the job of two eyes, fixing a moving three-dimensional object in space so that my hand could reach out and take hold of it. The technical term for this trick is accommodation. Normally, people need two eyes to make this happen, when the muscles controlling the shape of the eyeball – lengthening or shortening the optical distance between the lens and the retina – operate together so that the two images of the object looked at are transformed by the brain into a single 3-D picture. In my case, this magical transformation took place entirely inside my right eye; my left eye took no part in the process, instead wandering all over the place, often squinting at something over my left shoulder. I was too young to be distressed by this, although my mother must have been, to have given birth to a boss-eyed boy who looked like an imbecile. The optician provided me with a pair of spectacles, the right lens of which had been taped over so that my lazy eye would have to work. That was the theory. In practice, when I wore them I couldn't see and my head hurt. I could no longer catch balls or see near or far objects, make out even the red outline of the bus, let alone the number on the front of it. My left eye wasn't useless but it wasn't much good either. As soon as I was outside the garage, crossing Bayswater Road at the traffic lights, stalking my quarry through the undergrowth along the Serpentine, I found it convenient to keep my glasses in my pocket.

Dad decided I should see a specialist. For him that meant one thing: Harley Street. It would be hard to imagine my dad waiting his turn in a crowded outpatients' department of a National Health hospital, although it would be hard to imagine him waiting his turn under any circumstances. He shaved, put on a shirt and a collar, his RN tie and his blazer with gold RN buttons, his ox-blood polished brogues, found his teeth and chauffeured me in Old Mother Riley to a town house in Harley Street. There, a kindly old gentleman in a three-piece suit stood me in front of him and asked me to watch the chocolate grenadier in coloured silver paper as he moved it slowly to and fro across my line of vision. Then he sat me on a chair in front of a machine in which, when I looked into it, I saw a pink lion on the left side of my field of vision and a yellow cage on the right. In response to negative and affirmative prompts from me and small adjustments to the machine by the old gentleman, the lion could be persuaded to enter the cage. After this had been accomplished the old gentleman was so pleased with me he gave me the chocolate grenadier to eat. If he thought I was going to put it in my pocket and eat it later he was mistaken.

I don't know what he told Dad, probably that the remedy in a case as serious as mine was for me to have an eye transplant. To me he said that I had one of my dad's eyes and one of my mum's and I must learn to use both of them at the same time, instead of what I was doing, using now one, now the other. This explanation made perfect sense to me. Even then I knew that my mum and dad saw things differently to each other. In fact, was there a single subject they saw eye to eye on? Where to live. What kind of place to live in, in which part of the country. What sort of people they should have as friends. How to spend their money. Which station to tune the radio to, the Home Service or the Light Programme. If only they could come together permanently and reach an agreement about how to live their lives, as the parents of other children did, everything would be all right.

Although the kind old gentleman in Harley Street had put his finger on it, I continued to look at things through my right eye and, through my left, perceived a ghostly mosaic of images. It was useful to know that there was a world on the left side of my body but I tended to ignore it as I went about my business. I continued to catch balls, decipher bus numbers, peruse the *Beano* and to see the world through my dad's eye, rather than my mum's. With *her* eye I possessed a less literal vision that perceived a misty, dreamy domain where things were not as they seemed: left-handed, nebulous and numinous. One half of me saw the world with the heartless certainty of Colonel Custer marshalling his Winchester rifles before the tepees; the other saw it with the clarity of the blind Sioux squaw threading the scalps of the pony soldiers onto the war lance.

Who knows? If my mum and dad had been less incompatible, more accommodating towards each other, my two eyes might have learnt to work together. I might have looked at the world as people normally look at it, unambiguously, without the double vision I came to live with. As it was, my two eyes remained together and apart, as my mum and dad did.

Jenner

During the part of the day I roamed the north end of Kensington Gardens – between early morning and mid-afternoon, until the light faded – there were few people at large and, on weekdays, never other children. The empty paths were furred with frost and the white grass remained undisturbed until I chose to disturb it. The sky was battleship-grey and sometimes came all the way down to the ground so that a wispy fog concealed everything. On those mornings when a pale sun glimmered, it thawed the frost enough to leave the shapes of trees in white relief on the grass. In the Italian Garden the fountains were turned off and their basins, like four huge empty soup tureens, were eloquent of austerity. Jenner, seated in his high chair, brooding on the mysteries of contagion and inoculation, peered out of the mist. Now that the storm had abated, a misty stillness hung over the water, here and there stiff with ice. The storm debris-strewn grass, which seemed to have lost its novelty for the ladies and gentlemen in furs and smart overcoats, retained its allure for me. I didn't find the park dank or dismal, but others evidently did.

Entering Kensington Gardens was to leave the city, the world of houses, roads, cars, buses, dustcarts, Underground trains, the radio, the human factor. From the banks of the

Serpentine no building's silhouette broke the horizon in any direction, so you didn't feel you were inside the city but out of it. In the still air each small sound was amplified: water plashing against the wooden posts, on each one of which a gull perched; the soft conversation of rooks in the uppermost branches of the elms. Blackbirds and thrushes rummaged among the previous year's leaves. Ducks honked. I collected interesting items, which I kept in my pockets: berries the colour of blood, the hollow exoskeletons of insects, empty oak calyxes like spent cartridge cases, seeds that heltered and skeltered when tossed into the air. This was not only a different place; it was a different kind of place, an ancient zone in which time played no part, where a small boy was a giant and no mortal had authority over him. The bronze statue of a boy playing pan pipes in the company of fairies and squirrels I took to be a monument dedicated to the glory of myself.

So when I spied on the perimeter of the Italian Garden a person my own size, a girl settling her doll into her pram in the company of a young woman seated on one of the benches, I observed her from a safe distance, hidden behind the lip of a fountain basin in the vicinity of Jenner. Eyeing her with the patience of a hunter, one foot placed cautiously in front of the other, I sidled towards this interesting-looking person without glancing in her direction, as if my presence increasingly close to her was entirely fortuitous, until the young woman on the bench, whom I had forgotten to take account of, without looking up from what she was writing, called out:

'Hello, boy!'

I froze, aghast to find myself addressed, as if I had been caught red-handed doing something for which I might be punished. She looked up, met my eye and, at the sight of me, smiled.

'Well? Aren't you going to say hello?'

'Hello.'

'Are you on your own?'

My head nodded.

'Isn't your mother here?'

I did my best to look non-committal. I already understood, without quite knowing why, that there were pieces of information about myself it wasn't always in my interest to divulge. A habit I must have acquired from my dad.

'You mean, you're here on your own?'

'Yes, miss.'

'How old are you?'

'Six,' I lied.

'What's your name?'

'Neil Grant, miss.'

Grant was the name my father was living under at that time.

'Have you had mumps, Neil Grant?'

Unsure whether mumps was a sort of snack, like elevenses, I hesitated. I had been caught out like that before. But it wasn't a trick question. The girl, whose name was Lucy, was recovering from mumps which, the young woman explained to me, was a fairly serious illness, especially for boys, so I shouldn't come too close. This in itself was thrilling. If I touched this girl I would immediately catch something. She was dangerous and for that reason I was drawn to her, as I was involuntarily drawn to the live electric rail in the Underground.

After that, I saw Lucy almost every day over the following weeks. Like me she lived close by, although probably not in a converted garage. The beautiful young woman, it turned out, was not Lucy's mother but her sister, who came to the park to write letters in a leather writing case, holding the fountain pen in leather-gloved fingers. I didn't ask myself why she wrote her letters in the park and not at home, where she would be warm. I supposed she had a reason. Lucy and I played together and we became best friends. She was happy to take part in my adventures and to play hiding and chasing games. I looked forward to seeing her and she seemed to take for granted that I was always in the Gardens, waiting for her by the fountains, as if I lived there. To Lucy I was a marvellous boy with a bow and arrow, who was fearless and fleet of foot. To me she was the necessary adjunct to my kingdom, a princess with golden hair tied up behind with a ribbon, with shiny black shoes and a pretty dress under her sensible coat, white leggings under her dress. Her hair smelt of soap. In fact, everything about her was neat and clean, her hands and her clothes. Her face was without blemish. I found myself drawn to looking at her face, intrigued by it, in particular by the little indentation above her mouth, by her mouth itself, which changed from moment to moment. Her smile made me smile. Her skin fascinated me. She was a girl; that was the thing. Her girl's voice was delightful, especially when she laughed, and when she called my name across the cold flagstones *Neil! . . . Neil! . . . Come! Quick!* When Lucy called my name, I came. Quick.

With this companion to share my adventures, running at my side, I was complete.

Lucy's sister, once she had decided it was safe for us to fraternise, had given us permission to play together on condition we remained within the Italian Garden. She wrote on the sheets of paper on her lap while we stalked and chased. We fired arrows through the stone balustrade at sitting ducks on the Serpentine. We climbed down the duckboards into the empty fountain basins, played *Paul Temple and the Case of the Lost Girl.* We crept up behind wicked strangers who pretended not to see us. We marched her pram and doll past her sister with our noses in the air like a married couple taking a stroll with their new baby. In the ornate stone alcove that had been erected for the convenience of eighteenth-century ladies and gentlemen we ate the biscuits and cake her sister provided for Lucy and, in due course, for me, since I had brought nothing myself. I made up stories for her about myself, about the perils I protected her from and the secret place inside the trunk of a tree, hidden beyond where she was allowed to go. I hinted to her of its special magic and I should have liked to have been there with her, the two of us alone, eating our biscuits. I was careful not to divulge where this place was, which was a secret, although one day I would. One day I would take her there.

Lucy made a big impression on me, perhaps the first of its kind in my life. I experienced the usual symptoms. Although I didn't recognise them as such at the time, I would come to later: the day-dreaming about the person in her absence, the quickening of the pulse at her approach, the feeling of well-being in her presence. The desire to look at her and to be looked at by her. Only when her eyes were upon me, her voice calling my name, did I understand what it meant *to be*.

Then one day Lucy and her sister failed to appear. I waited. They did not come. Nor did they come the next day. I was baffled at first, then glum, then cross, then glum again. I visited the deserted fountains at the time of day she was usually there, looking for her – every day I paced the cold flagstones with my sword, waiting for her to appear – but she never returned. Lucy had gone for ever. All that remained of the girl were a few fugitive swatches of memory: the colour of her dress, the indentation above her mouth, the sound of her voice calling to me across the deserted fountains, the soapy smell of her hair. For a time I carried these fragmentary recollections around with me like the exoskeletons of insects and seeds in my pocket until, like them, they disintegrated into nothing.

So it was true, what her sister had warned me about Lucy: she *had* been dangerous. She had touched me and I had caught something. Dear old Jenner had been no protection.

Lucy

On Sunday mornings, during our walk in Kensington Gardens and back through Hyde Park before opening time at the V&A, we made a clockwise circuit of the Round Pond – which, Dad liked to point out, is neither round nor a pond. As well as the men with their beautiful scale working models of ocean-going yachts navigating the choppy water, there were also men who came to the open space between the Pond and the bandstand to fly their kites. These were not children's kites but serious box kites almost the size of the men who flew them. They stood apart from each other, leaning back against the pull of the line that linked them to the tiny object high up in the sky.

I had a small Woolworth's sailing boat we sometimes sailed across the Round Pond – which it did do eventually – but it was the kites that interested Dad. He knew how yachts worked and how close to sheet the mainsail of my little boat in the prevailing meteorological conditions. How kites remained airborne was more of a mystery to him.

While I sailed my boat, he fell into conversation with one of the kite-flyers. By the time I returned, the tiny red speck in the sky had become a huge red object on the ground. Dad was quizzing the owner of the object about the aerodynamics of his canvas-and-wood assemblage. On the way home he put it to me: 'I think we should build ourselves a kite. What do you think?'

I couldn't think of anything in the world I should like more.

Over the following week he made a scale drawing, a smaller version of a kite we had seen: a pair of open-ended boxes joined by parallel axes of wood. Each day at tea time, after he had finished his own work, he set about making the drawings a reality. He knelt on the carpet near the paraffin stove and I knelt beside him while he thought of ways to affix to each other quarter-inch square spars of timber. Instead of canvas he chose the strong opaque paper he used for his drawings that blueprints were made from, which was impossible to tear. My job was to follow his instructions and pass him the tools he needed. I was enthralled. While he worked, he talked, as he always talked, as if I could understand half of what he was talking about.

'April the sixteenth, 1912 – it so happens I can tell you the exact day – my brothers and I were on top of Pirn Crag. It was a marvellous, blowy morning with high, fast-moving cumulus clouds in a blue sky: perfect weather for kite-flying. Duncan and Ian were with me so it must have been during the Easter holiday. I was at a ghastly prep school in Essex, on the Blackwater, and they were also in England, borders at King's School in Worcester, so we were all probably glad to be let off the leash. I was overjoyed to have them home. I worshipped my brothers. They were like gods to me. Ian played wing three-quarters for the Colts and Duncan already had a motorcycle, a 3½-horsepower Rudge-Whitworth that cost £46. But they were both very easy with me. There was no rank-pulling or teasing. They loved me in a way no one loved me, not even Mother. Only Toshie, my wet nurse, loved me as much as my brothers loved me.

'Anyway, Ian had dug out the old kites he had used when he was my age and, to fly them, we had climbed Pirn Crag, the highest land formation in the vicinity – called Pirn Crag, by the way, because of its shape. A *pirn* is the spool of a shuttle in a loom. The only factories in the area were the Tweed mills, which made tartans. When you remember that half the British army then wore tartan you can see why there was so much money about.'

'How old were you?'

'Ten. Wait. What am I talking about? Nine! My birthday wasn't until September.

'We climbed Pirn Crag and flew the kites and it was terrific fun. I didn't know at the time, of course, that these moments would turn out to be among the happiest in my life. How could I have known that then?

'We had wound the kites in and we were sitting on the top of Pirn Crag, getting our breath back. The view up there on such a clear day was like nothing on earth. You could see for miles. Traquair Forest, the Tweed winding between the Lowlands. It gave you an immensely good feeling. I can't remember which of us saw it first: a thing hanging in the air some way to the south. It was a golden eagle, Ian said. There were still golden eagles nesting that far south in those days, although I had never seen one myself.

'"No it isn't," Duncan said. "I'll be damned if it's not an aeroplane!"

'Which is what it was. This queer-looking, delicate assemblage of wood and wire coming our way was a monoplane. God knows what it was doing there. The Daily Mail Round Britain Air Race, that had included Edinburgh, had been held a couple of years before but there was no race this year. Duncan, who understood such matters, declared it to be a

Blériot, since nearly all the other aeroplanes then were bi- or even triplanes.

'The closer she came, the more wonderful she looked. We were quite high up, you see, not all that far below the aircraft. And we could hear her too now. The steady turning of the engine didn't sound so very different to Duncan's Rudge-Whitworth. She was flying slowly into the wind in the direction of Minchmuir and the Tweed at – what? – fifty, sixty miles per hour? She was on course for Edinburgh, it looked like.

'None of us had seen an aeroplane airborne before, so it was enormously exciting. We had seen pictures of all the latest models in magazines and we knew the names of the famous aviators – Americans and Frenchmen, for the most part. To see an actual aircraft in flight and almost at eye-level was something beyond our wildest dreams. Well, we waved like mad, trying our best to attract the pilot's attention, because we could see him clearly as he approached. Then, when he was almost level, he noticed us. I can see his face today, his moustache, his scarf and his flying-goggles. But instead of waving to us, he seemed to bow from the waist and give us a rather formal salute with his gloved hand. He must have been foreign, French probably.

'We watched the machine and listened to the glorious sound of the engine until, though our senses strained, both sight and sound faded and eventually disappeared. She was gone and the tranquillity of the rolling landscape returned: the sky returned to how it had been. We, however, had been changed for ever. Seeing a Blériot under such circumstances, in each other's company, meant everything to us. On impromptu occasions thereafter – on parade before church or behind Mr Watt's back while he was reading *The Times* to the servants – one of us three would give the aviator's slow, august salute to the other two, bowing from the waist. We considered it the height of savoir faire . . .'

Our kite was coming on. The frame was ready and Dad was considering different methods of attaching the drawing paper to it. Should he use pin tacks or glue? Before he fixed the paper panels to the frame he suggested I might like to paint them. His drawing paper was made to repel water and so, using Dad's coloured drawing inks, I painted scenes of trees and birds and a boy flying a kite.

'You've made a bloody mess of that,' my dad said when he saw my efforts. 'Never mind. It'll do.'

He wrapped the panels around the frame and glued and tacked them and the thing began to look like a kite.

'What shall we call her, then?' he said.

Dad liked all machines, especially ships and cars, to have a name, preferably the name of a girl because, he maintained, girls and machines have a lot in common. They both need a lot of love and attention. You have to take good care of them because, if you don't, they will almost certainly play up.

'*Lucy*,' I said.

'That's a good name. We'll call her *Lucy*, shall we?'

'Yes, please.'

'We'll fly her on Sunday. I'll have to get hold of some fine line. Fishing line might do.'

'. . . Cock-a-hoop at our good fortune, we sprinted down the side of the crag to the Tweed, ran along the back riverside path under the old cedar trees and through the fruit garden to the House. We ran into one of the men and, all at the same time, quizzed him whether he had seen what we had seen – which he could easily have done, had he happened to look into the sky in the direction of Walkerburn at the crucial moment. But no, he had seen nothing unusual. He looked at us as if he thought we were mad, insofar as a servant can give such a look to the offspring of his employer. We interrogated each of the servants we met but none of them had a clue what we were talking about. In fact, they were decidedly odd. It was peculiar. We knew *we* had changed but it seemed to us that the House had changed too, while we had been away, into another House which was identical in every respect to the one we had left, except that in this one no one smiled nor looked at all pleased to see us.

'The family had already assembled – they were already seated at table for luncheon – when we burst into the dining room through the servants' door from the scullery where we had hastily washed our hands. We were brought up short immediately. The atmosphere was awful. Everyone was present: as well as Mother and Mr Watt and my sisters, Miss Blacker and Mother's maids, my nurse Toshie, even old Gregory, the head gardener, standing in his stockinged feet. Nobody was speaking, which was unheard of in our house, where everyone spoke at once. We boys sat down and waited. Mr Watt, instead of scolding us for our late and indecorous entry, put on his spectacles and, before saying Grace, gave us the news from the morning's edition of *The Times*: the *Titanic* had sunk.

'Mr Watt read out the details that were known then. She had struck a growler in the night. Had gone down in under three hours. Hundreds were feared lost. Survivors had been picked up by an American ship, the *Carpathia*, whose assistance had been summoned by Marconi's new radiography system.

'The largest ship ever to be built had sunk on her maiden voyage. It was the greatest shipping disaster in history. We were stunned. Mother clasped her napkin to her breast. Several of the servants wept. My sisters probably wanted to weep but they knew it was their duty to set an example.

'We'd all read about the *Titanic*, of course, and we were terribly proud of her, even if she'd not been built on the Clyde but in Belfast. The *Titanic*, you see, proved something about us: we could do anything we set our mind to. We ruled the waves. We built the best ships in the world and our best one had just sunk. It wasn't only a tragedy for all the poor blighters who had gone down with her, whole streets of Southampton, it was a National Tragedy. To tell the truth, I wasn't all that interested in the fate of the poor blighters who had gone down; it was the ship I cared about. What a terrible thing to have happened – to *us*! In terms of international prestige it was the equivalent of taking sterling off the gold standard.

'It was a bloody shock, I can tell you. We hadn't seen it coming, although we should have done – as Captain Smith should have seen the growler. We didn't understand what it *meant*. It was an omen, if we'd had the sense to see it as such. In a couple of years the British Empire would strike its own growler. Within a generation it would sink without a trace almost as rapidly as the *Titanic* had done.

'The house went into mourning. Family, friends, servants, spoke in low voices; no games were allowed. Slowly over the following days more details emerged. There had been too few lifeboats on board to save everybody. The American millionaires had behaved impeccably. Jacob Aster, the richest man in the world, had declined a seat in the last boat to be lowered. Captain Smith had gone down with his ship, along with his Newfoundland hound, Luath. In the kirk on Sunday the vicar probably spoke from his pulpit on the tragedy. He probably read a text that attempted to make the unsinkable thinkable. I can't remember. Whatever text he chose, it almost certainly wasn't Pride Precedes a Fall.

'Wherever you went – in the village, at home, later at school – it was all anyone talked about. Nobody was interested in hearing about the fabulous machine three brothers had seen on top of Pirn Crag.

'Did it put me off a maritime career? I'll say it did! Even if – as the youngest son – my name had been put down for Osborne, the last thing I wanted to be was a bloody sailor. Far from it! I was going to be an aviator!'

As was his custom on our Sunday morning walk, Dad was in his best togs – his Navy greatcoat over his blazer, clean shirt, cufflinks, pressed trousers, ox-blood brogues, and a piece of silk around his neck in the colours of his term at Dartmouth. From Kensington Gardens we would head straight for the Victoria and Albert to be there at midday, opening time, and he liked to look the part of the person he was playing in the stories he told about himself. Although Dad enjoyed pubs and he spent a lot of time in them, he wasn't a great drinker. He drank half pints of ordinary bitter. It wasn't the opportunity to consume alcohol he sought in the private bar of a public house but to perform, to tell stories to the Gang. According to Mum, the Gang only listened to his stories because he was first to put his hand in his pocket to pay for a round. *Spongers* was what she called them behind his back. To his face, it was guaranteed to put the cat among the pigeons.

Dad carried our kite to the place where the kite-flyers congregated near the bandstand and he found the chap he had spoken to the previous Sunday. A stiff breeze was tousling the grass, making rapid runic shapes on the surface of the Round Pond.

'I like the paintings,' the chap said. 'Did *you* do them?'

I nodded. I was too excited to speak.

'What kind of line do you have?' he asked Dad.

'Some kitchen yarn I found knocking about.'

The kite man looked doubtful.

'The drag on the line is exponential to the height of the kite,' the man said.

'Is it, by God? So it might not hold?'

The kite man shrugged.

'It'll hold,' he said. 'Up to a point.'

He showed us how to attach the line, first making a pair of bridles from the spars and joining these to the line.

I held the kite while Dad walked backwards, unwinding the line. I held her high above my head. After several vain attempts at throwing her into the air, a gust took our *Lucy* which, straining against the line, suddenly released herself into the sky. Dad played out the line and up she went. Up and up.

I danced. I shouted with glee. Our funny-looking earthbound construction was in the air! Dad was delighted too. For me, *Lucy* was a kite; for Dad, she was a scientific experiment.

'Here! Take her!'

Dad handed me the stick the line was wound around. I took it in both hands and the frisky tug of the kite, like an animal at the end of a lead, surprised me, dragging me a few steps, as if the kite was holding on to me, rather than the reverse. I had to fight the urge to release the stick, which was what I really wanted to do, not to stop *Lucy* from soaring ever higher. Then, without warning, the weight pulling against my body was no longer there. The line had gone slack. In fact, the line had gone altogether. At first I didn't understand what had happened. The line, extended to its entire length, had run out because the end had not been attached to the stick. Dad and the kite chap were laughing at the look on my face.

It was all over. We watched the two little squares sail upwards until they disappeared over Park Lane. For me it was a moment of mixed emotions: of sadness and triumph. Something had ended and something else had begun – but what?

Dad, who was delighted with the result of his aeronautical experiment, shook hands with the kite man and set off in the direction of the pub. On the way, he was silent. I could almost hear him thinking. He had not built the kite for my amusement, of course, but for his own. He had wanted to see how high she would fly in the prevailing meteorological conditions.

Although *Lucy* was gone for ever, we were both, for our different reasons, happy. He had successfully defied gravity. I had let her go.

Begbie

Ian Begbie, who had only a single bed-sitting room to call home, was a regular visitor to the garage. It was no surprise to wake up in the morning and find him asleep under a blanket between the two armchairs. Before he opened his bloodshot eyes, I often made a close inspection of his person: his thinning, colourless hair; the hairs on his bumpy earlobes; his gaping mouth with its uneven discoloured teeth; his bristly chin and sunken cheeks. I breathed in his distinctive pong. I was both repelled and delighted to be able to inspect from close quarters a grown-up with such fascinatingly unappealing facial parts. Had this person not been Begbie, a man I knew to be harmless, gentle in his dealings with me – in fact, excessively courteous to everyone – I should have been frightened. I wasn't in the least frightened. Of all Dad's chums, I loved Begbie best of all.

Dad enjoyed Begbie's company, tolerating his grubby cuffs and dishevelled appearance, even though the man shared none of his own preoccupations. Begbie had no technical interests, quite the reverse; he disagreed with Dad about the importance of maths and science, which he considered to be merely tools, like a fountain pen or a pair of scissors, to be put to use for good or ill. The atom bomb – pictures of which were in all the newspapers – proved Begbie's point.

No it didn't; it proved Dad's. They liked to argue the toss about such matters over cups of tea after the pub had shut on Sunday afternoon and we had shared our slices of fried corned beef on toast with him. They discussed politics and history and told each other stories about *Before the War* and *During the War*, which usually sent me to sleep. It was the one thing they had in common: an interest in narrative. With his quiet, donnish way of expressing himself, Begbie was the perfect foil for Dad's mercurial, impetuous temperament. One reason Dad liked having him around was because he was such a good listener. While they talked, I doodled on scraps of paper on the carpet on the floor between their knees, next to the paraffin heater, comforted by the incomprehensible murmur of their conversation.

Even though he had a degree from Cambridge and had fought in the War in some capacity or other, Begbie had no proper job and he was nearly always short of cash. There was no Mrs Begbie. He never talked about what he did, as if what he did was something that reflected badly on him, which he was ashamed of and ought not to be spoken of in public – although Dad was happy to enlighten any third party. Begbie was a member of a profession that aroused neither approval nor interest but a kind of bored dismay. He was a poet.

A poet was a writer whose words didn't reach all the way to the edge of the page.

Begbie's bed-sitting room, which I visited with Dad a few times, was at the top of four grubby flights of stairs in a town house in Inverness Terrace that had fallen on bad times. Each of the rooms of the main staircase was occupied by a different tenant, any of whom you might meet on your way up. After we had negotiated the four landings, Begbie, in his dressing-gown, opened his door to us and invited us in. The room, which gave off an even stronger whiff of Begbie's distinctive pong, was, like him, scruffy and unclean, the bed unmade, his trousers folded over the back of a chair. What was unexpected and delightful was the enormous number of books that were arranged neatly in piles on the floor and along shelves up the walls. The neat arrangement of the books was in contrast with the general dishevelment of the rest of the room. On a desk in front of the window was a portable typewriter and some typed sheets of paper and more books. Dad owned a few books, a complete set of *Encyclopaedia Britannica*, for example, and some heavy tomes that consisted solely of column after column of numbers. But these were reading books, some with pictures in them, others with leather bindings. This was what Begbie spent his money on: second-hand books from street markets and jumble sales. He picked up interesting editions for pennies in Portobello Road and Chapel Street Market and exchanged them for pound notes in Charring Cross Road. He was a man who lived by words, reading and writing them, buying and selling them. It seemed a pretty good sort of job to me.

Begbie, when he dropped by the garage, nearly always produced from his pocket a children's book he had brought along for me: *The Flower Fairies*, *Milly Molly Mandy*, *The Story of Little Black Sambo*. Some of the books had pictures, others words I wasn't able to read. These Begbie read to me himself while Dad was finishing off in his cubbyhole:

Tweedle Dum and Tweedle Dee
Agreed to have a battle;
For Tweedle Dum said Tweedle Dee
Had spoiled his brand-new rattle.

'Again!'

After Begbie had recited the poem a few times I knew it by heart myself.

'Who is Tweedle Dum?' I asked him.

'Don't you know?'

'No. Who is he?'

'I think you do. *And* Tweedle Dee?'

'No, I don't!'

'Who was sitting in that armchair this afternoon?'

'You!'

'And who was sitting in this one?'

'Dad!'

'And what were we doing?'

'I don't know. Quarrelling?'

'Tweedle Dum and Tweedle Dee.'

'Are you Tweedle Dum?'

Begbie looked indignant.

'Certainly *not*! *I* am Tweedle-*Dee*!'

The reason we went round to Begbie's room was to drag him out of his dressing gown, oblige him to put on his trousers and hat and coat and accompany us on our Sunday morning walk around the Pond. Then, at least, Dad told him, we would arrive at the V&A with oxygen in our lungs. Begbie joined us without enthusiasm. Even before we had completed our circuit of the Gardens he was out of breath. We sat down on the enclosed bench near the statue of Queen Victoria, in front of Kensington Palace. On this breezy March morning the little arbour was a sun trap. I lolled between them while Dad prepared his pipe and Begbie, from Dad's tin, his, enveloped in the sweet aroma of Sobranie tobacco smoke.

'. . . I was thirteen when I joined the Navy – which is what you do when you go to Osborne, and then, if you pass the exam, Dartmouth. With my eldest brother Duncan already dead in France – a lieutenant in the KOSBs – and the way things were going there, the army was out. Mr Watt persuaded Mother to send me to Osborne. It was the done thing then for good families to let the Navy have the youngest son. I sat my entry exam in February 1916 and went up in May – in the same term, by the way, as George Saxe-Coburg-Gotha, youngest son of the king, brother of the Prince of Wales. Louis Battenberg – Mountbatten to you – was in the term above ours.

'In April I joined Ian at Brighton, where he was on leave. Because Duncan was dead, we were glad to be with each other. Ian didn't want me to put on a long face and so I did my best not to. He'd be back in the line soon enough, so he didn't want to mope. I walked alongside Captain Ferguson of the Royal Scots in my newly tailored naval cadet uniform, proud as Punch, saluting officers who outranked him, declining to salute those who didn't. I hadn't the foggiest idea what a Navy salute looked like then. What those staff types thought of this pipsqueak saluting them I hate to think. After my visit, when he put me on the London train, from the platform he solemnly gave me the Blériot aviator's august salute.

'On the tenth of May Mother saw me off in a special train from Victoria at 8 a.m. She herself took the *Scotsman* back to Waverley from King's Cross. The next day, about the time I was falling in for the first time on Portsmouth jetty, Ian was killed in Belgium – a year after Duncan, almost to the day – although it was weeks before I was told the news by the Old Man, Captain Holmes à Court. In those days boys weren't supposed to blub under these circumstances, but I did. I had loved my brothers. They were all I had.'

'You lost *both* of them?'

'I did, Begbie. Both.'

'My God! And how old was Ian?'

'Eighteen. At his death, he was the youngest captain in the regiment.'

'How dreadful! It must have been terrible for you. How did you take it?'

'Badly. I was bloody angry. I blamed everyone for their deaths, from the king down. It scarred me for life.'

'I should think it would.'

'Mother never got over it. She closed up the house and moved to Edinburgh, to a dreary grey building in Polwarth Terrace, where she sat behind lace curtains for the rest of her days. Dada was already in his grave in his own kirk, don't forget, so there were no men left – except me, and I wasn't a man. The family affairs, Dada's estate, drifted into the hands of Mr Watt, a canny old Morningside lawyer whom mother trusted, and he soon had his feet under the table. Servants were let go. My sister Mary was in black for her young man, Robyn Welsh, late of the Scots Guards. There was many a poor girl in her position, I can tell you. Too bloody many.

'I finished up Cadet Captain of my term more because of my maths and drawing than my seamanship. But it meant I was given a plum posting. I was sent to the Med where I was taken on at Malta as midshipman on *Ajax*, a King George V class battleship. We steamed to the Black Sea with her sister ship *Centurion*. Don't ask me what we were doing there. Control of the Dardanelles has always been at the heart of British policy towards the Russians. We poked our nose into everyone's business then.

'Well, we were lying off the Crimea, between Sevastopol and Yalta . . .'

'When would this be?'

'This would be in 1919. The Reds had swept all before them but the Whites still had an army, even if Trotsky had it bottled up in Georgia. Lloyd George had landed some sailors and troops but they were pretty ineffectual. It's nearly always the case that regulars will underestimate a people's militia during a revolution. Anyway, there we were, standing off Cape Sarych, flying the flag, twiddling our thumbs, enjoying the caviar, which was ludicrously cheap. It had become a question now of taking off as many of the Imperial Entourage that we could ferry to Constant. Once Odessa fell, the situation became hopeless.

'It must have been a Sunday, after Divisions and Church on quarterdeck because the ratings were in Number Ones and the wardroom in frock coats, cocked hats and swords; we midshipmen in bum-freezers and wearing dirks. Mediterranean summer whites, all of us. Suddenly, consternation overcame the ratings forward and those about to leave the quarterdeck rushed to the side. We all squinnied landwards to where four individuals could be seen swimming our way. We were lying a couple of miles out from the shore and these people had swum almost half that distance. They were waving. It wasn't possible to make out who they were.

'The commander had the picket-boat called away and he put me in to cox it. Told me to go and fetch the bloody fools and bring them aboard. He had his glasses on them so he was in a position to see who they were.

'The men rowed out to the quartet and we took on board three exhausted young ladies and a stout middle-aged fellow. It wasn't easy. You have to manhandle a person in the water to get him – or her – into a small boat without capsizing it. In order to swim out the ladies had sensibly removed their stockings and skirts. They had on their white cotton bodices and bloomers but as they came out of the water they might just as well have been naked. What a sight they made!

'I took off my jacket and had a couple of the men remove their matelot tops to cover these lovely sea creatures. We turned about and rowed back to the ship, the men grinning from ear to ear. The girls too.

'Well, you can imagine. The entire ship's complement, even the stokers from the engine room, had turned out to greet this little party: three pretty young ladies in soaking wet drawers! It wasn't a sight often seen on the deck of one of His Majesty's fighting ships, believe me. A snotty was dispatched below, reappearing with an armful of dressing-gowns and the party was discretely ushered from the shameless gaze of the men.'

'Well, I never!' Begbie said.

'You might have thought that I had played my part in this little diversion but there was more to come. The Russian chap identified himself as one General Kozlov – and he had an official brevet in an oilskin wallet to prove it. These lovelies were his daughters. But that was as far as it went. None of the Russians spoke a word of English. They spoke beautiful French, of course, but in the Royal Navy speaking any foreign language was frowned upon and to speak French practically a flogging offence. This is where my services were required again, because it was known that I – for my sins – spoke the language fluently.

'That evening I was invited – *invited*, mind, not ordered! – to attend dinner with the commander in the wardroom, where our guests were assembled in a motley of Navy garments. The three sisters were absolutely delightful, chirruping in their own lingo like parakeets, and the general himself was a rum character, perfectly at ease among fellow officers. I was there to translate for both parties, which I did until the ladies were invited to retire so that the port could be passed. Before taking our leave, each one took me in her arms and kissed me on both cheeks, in the French manner.

'Over the port and cigars the general expressed his gratitude to me for my gallantry in the whaler. He enquired of the commander – through me, of course – if he had any objection to him awarding me a decoration on behalf of His Imperial Majesty. It wasn't widely known yet that the Romanovs and their brood had already been shot by the Bolsheviks. Well, the commander shrugged. He couldn't give two hoots. The general took down my name and rank and solemnly declared with the authority invested in him by His Imperial Majesty Nicholas II, Tsar of all the Russians, that I was to be the honoured recipient of the Order of St Catherine (Third Class).

'I never thought any more about it – until a year later, when I was in the Aegean, serving on HMS *Centurion*. I received a package from Paris that contained a letter in French and Russian and a bloody great gold gong with an orange and black ribbon!

'For a dare, I wore it on my Number Ones on Sunday at Divisions. The midshipman sub didn't see the funny side. He almost tossed it into the drink and me after it!'

'So there you are, Begbie, since you ask. *That's* the story of how I came by it.'

Begbie clapped his hands.

'Splendid, Luke! Splendid! What a delightful tale!'

'Damn thing wasn't real gold, of course. Not even gold plate. I tried to hock it in Liverpool years later when I was on my beam ends. The man wouldn't give me ten bob for it. I let him have it for seven and six.'

Begbie, crumpled up between the two leather armchairs pushed together, eventually opened his bloodshot eyes. Without moving his head, he looked at me and smiled his lizard-like, yellow-toothed smile, which was on level with the stub-filled ashtray on the arm of the chair.

'Hello, my boy. What time is it?'

I brought him the clock. I couldn't tell the time. Begbie looked at the clock and said under his breath: 'The wind is old and still at play, And I must hurry on my way.'

Because it was a weekday, he knew that it would be best if he made himself scarce. The last thing Dad wanted was a pub chum hanging around when he was about to get down to work. It made him short-tempered. Begbie retrieved his spectacles from inside his shoes, put on his tie and made himself a pot of tea. He lit a cigarette. While he drank his tea and smoked his cigarette, with his fountain pen, in his beautifully neat handwriting, he wrote a note to Dad on a piece of graph paper he found lying about. Before letting himself out, he held the curtain to one side for me while I carried in a cup of tea to Dad. I shook Dad's arm until he woke.

'Is that tea there?' he growled.

'Yes.'

'Has Begbie gone?'

'Yes.'

'Good!'

After Dad had dressed and washed and we had had our porridge, he found Begbie's note. He looked at it for some time, muttered 'Hmn!' and then put it to one side and headed for his drawing board to start his day's work. Later he must have tucked it into one of the volumes of the *Encyclopaedia Britannica*, which was where he kept things he didn't know what to do with but didn't want to throw away. The note remained where he had put it until the person who ended up in possession of the encyclopaedias, many years later, long after the death of Tweedle Dum and Tweedle Dee, opened that particular volume and a slip of graph paper came to hand:

And at the foot of the rainbow we tear
its roots from our hearts with fingers
driven by cowardice and despair,
that its awful splendour
will not linger
here, but leave us to the ordinariness
that we prefer.

Gloucester Terrace

In April Dad found a proper flat, the ground floor of a no-longer-smart Victorian building in Gloucester Terrace, which in those days formed one side of a parallelogram with Westbourne Terrace that ended in Bayswater Road, where our mews was. As someone who made his living out of solid geometry, he must have enjoyed the Euclidean symmetry of this. As well as being cheap, two pounds-odd a week, the new place had the advantage that he could move into it without interrupting his social life. It was within striking distance of his haunts. He could walk to the V&A for lunch in under five minutes and be back at his drawing board in the same amount of time. He could visit his friends Begbie and Zoltan. Gordon and Doreen had a flat in the same street, the posh end. The thing about moving into number 36a was that Dad didn't have to leave Bayswater. It also meant my mum would be able to join us with my sister and, in due course, my brother, from wherever they had been parked. We would soon be a family again.

My mother and my sister had been parked in a place called Traquair, which was in Scotland. I never learnt where my brother had been. I later supposed he had been taken to a secret place in order to acquire special powers.

My mother, when Dad and I met her and my sister at King's Cross, was wearing a black beret on the side of her head and, under her fur coat, a fitted black cotton frock with a re-embroidered red, green and gold spaghetti pattern on it. Slim and lovely against the exhilaratingly noisy steam train she had just alighted from, which was called *The Flying Scotsman*, she looked like a film star. With her red lips and soft wavy hair, she was the most beautiful woman I had ever seen. I was satisfied she was the same person I had left three months before because I recognised her laugh and, once she had swept me up into her arms and given me a squeeze, her delicious lily-of-the-valley perfume. Only after I had been enveloped by the warmth of her body did I realise how cold I was.

About my sister – with her pretty dress and shiny black shoes, her pigtails and National Health specs, the pink version of the pair I was wearing myself – I kept an open mind. Three years older than me, she was taller, neater, cleaner – and she was a girl. I hadn't retained a clear enough picture of what she looked like to know whether or not she might have been switched for a similar fair-haired girl of the same height and age. We looked at each other sideways.

For a few days we continued to live in the garage. The new flat needed some work done to it before we could move in. It had come unfurnished so there were hardly any fixtures or fittings. We needed everything: beds, cupboards, tables, chairs, an ironing-board, a kettle, cups and saucers. The walls were dusty and damp, the cream-painted wallpaper retaining the shapes of removed pictures and mirrors; the lino was cracked. Dad had already cluttered up the place with his own stuff: his collection of disassembled electrical appliances, his tools, his bits of car engine that were going to come in useful one day, his *Encyclopaedia Britannica*, his drawing board and log tables. His sky-blue Staedtler pencils. Mum took one look at it all and burst into tears, which was not the reaction to their good fortune Dad had anticipated. Cross, he asked her what the bloody hell she expected for two pound seven and six a week in central London. A suite in Claridge's?

You reached the front door up a black and white tiled flight of stairs onto a portico supported by a pair of miniature Doric columns. Pieces of stucco were falling away from the columns and several of the tiles were cracked or missing. The front door opened onto a cream and brown corridor we shared with other occupants. Our flat was on the ground floor. The sitting room looked out onto the railings and a terrace identical to ours on the opposite side of the road. Number 36a was no more run down than any of the other buildings in the street. They all looked like this. Not all that long before, thousands of tons of high explosive had been dropped on them nightly. The Bishop's Bridge Road end of Gloucester Terrace, for example, wasn't even there.

Mum – who had been away from London throughout the winter to avoid the pea-soupers that would have aggravated her bronchitis – rolled her sleeves up and got down to work. My sister and I rolled our sleeves up and got down to work with her. Now the family was together in the same place, all Mum wanted was to make a nice home and have some things she could be proud of: a modern kitchen, a clean bathroom, some good bed linen. Cutlery that wasn't odd. New gas heaters, not coal fires she had to clear the ashes out of with a shovel every morning on her hands and knees and light with rolled-up copies of the *Manchester Guardian*, placing a single sheet over the front of the fire to make it draw until it scorched, caught alight and flew up the chimney. Mum's ambitions were modest. They were modest, lower-middle class ambitions, just the kind Dad tended to pooh-pooh.

One day a boy in long trousers walked through the door. Taller than my sister, stronger than me, cleverer than both of us, my brother occupied more space than we did together and he ate enough for two. We had to budge up to make room for him. He was a force to be reckoned with, someone who knew what was what. Until I met him I thought I knew a thing or two but I soon found out that I didn't know much about anything. When you told him something you thought he might be interested to hear, it turned out he already knew about it. He knew about birds, animals, aircraft – military and civil – the movement of the planets, cricket, mathematics; how to make things, how to whistle, climb trees, thread a conker, bounce stones on water. Since there was nothing he didn't know, you could never surprise him with some interesting piece of information. He was hard to impress.

But we rubbed along together. He didn't throw his weight around. In fact, he seemed to want to be my friend. Sometimes he rubbed along with Dad; other times he didn't and then Dad shouted at him. Dad shouted at all of us when we got in his way, including Mum. We were all still coming to terms with the fact that we were in a family. We were polite to each other, like people in a boarding-house trying to recall where we had seen the other guests before, wondering if they would be staying long. We were all different with different views about what was proper. We had different table manners – or none at all, in my case. Our accents were different. The one thing we had in common was a wariness of Dad, whom my brother called the Old Man. Dad was a much more difficult person to live with, I discovered, when he had to share a home with other members of my family than he had been living with me on my own.

The arrival of my brother introduced into the family a powerful magnetic force that pulled in the opposite direction to that exerted by my dad. Sensible, careful, respectful of authority, my brother found himself at odds with the cavalier risk-taker who governed us. Hereafter, my allegiance alternated between them like an electric current between opposing terminals: the caution of one and the dash of the other. Although I coveted the knowledge my brother possessed, I wanted to tell stories like my dad. To choose one was to refuse the other. There was no middle way. In time I came to understand that in the struggle between these two mighty adversaries, my allegiance was the prize.

The move to Gloucester Terrace had one unwelcome consequence for me: I was sent to school. I started at St Mary Abbots Church of England School on the corner of Kensington Church Street and Kensington High Street. Holding my brother's hand as we cut across the park, over Millionaire's Row and down the snicket off Holland Street, I was led to the gates of the Infants like a donkey. In a cruel twist of fate, I was no longer master of my own destiny, captain of all I beheld in the plains and avenues of Kensington Gardens, custodian of its secret places, practically a Lost Boy. I was a bigger boy's younger brother, a person he was responsible for.

At a stroke two other children were lodging with me – both of them cleverer and bigger than me; who knew how to count money, where to get on a bus and where to get off. Between them, they taught me to appreciate which side my bread was buttered on. Although I had no way of understanding it at the time, the best of my childhood was over.

But I found that I enjoyed school. One day you cooked

biscuits which, after they had cooled, you were allowed to eat. Another day you did nature study in the park – or music-and-movement in the hall. After we had collected seeds and feathers and leaves in Kensington Gardens, Miss Blythe gave us permission to dry our gloves along the brass rail of the guard in front of the open coal fire. She gave us coloured pencils, paint and brushes, sticky paper, scissors, glue, for us to make pictures out of the things we had collected. She gave each of us a nasturtium seed and a terracotta pot to plant it in. She told us to take the pot home, plant the seed in some earth and water it; to be careful not to water it too much. At the end of the school year we were to bring the pot back to be judged and she would award a prize for the best nasturtium flower in the class.

Miss Blythe liked me and I liked her. I wasn't clever but I would do anything to please Miss Blythe.

My brother was in his last year at this school, studying for his 11-plus exam. He had a girlfriend called Wendy Ball. He was a Boy Scout. He had a troop scarf and a woggle and a flat-brimmed bush hat, as well as a cleft stick for trapping snakes. He had a horn-handled sheath knife that he fastened onto his Scout belt, and an old yellow cricket bat called Jessop. He was the sort of talented handsome youth you would expect to grow up to be head boy of his school, captain of the cricket team, win a scholarship to Oxford, marry the prettiest girl there, have lots of babies and live happily ever after. After coming home from school and demolishing half a loaf of bread, washed down with a pint of milk, he would hop on to a 16 bus up the Edgware Road to Lord's to catch the last twenty overs of a Middlesex match – from four-thirty to stumps admittance to the ground was free to schoolboys – although Surrey was the team he supported.

After he passed his 11-plus exam he would go to a grammar school, so while he prepared for his exam he didn't have much time for me. I didn't blame him. I was half his age. He wasn't unfriendly to me. I was too small to be worth pushing around and, we both knew, I would never be as good as him at anything, so we weren't in competition with each other. He allowed me to cut out the action photographs from the *Daily Mirror* and the *Manchester Guardian* – 'Lock at second slip, diving to his right, catches Washbrook off Laker' – for him to stick into his green baize-covered cricket scrapbook. He gave me a threepenny bit to linseed his bat. But it was obvious I couldn't keep up with him. I had to settle for second best. As the two youngest in the family, my sister and I found it expedient to make a common cause with each other against the older, more powerful members.

My sister was a different kettle of fish to my brother, a much more complicated figure. She was three years younger than he was but she had the advantage over him of being a girl. He knew things; she knew different things. He was cleverer than both of us put together but in the end he was only a boy, like me. He knew much more than she did – long division, his times tables, the height of Mount Everest in feet, how to build a de Havilland Tiger Moth out of wood and tissue paper and then fly it. But my sister, who was left-handed, knew different, left-handed things. She sought the answer to questions it would never have occurred to my brother or me to ask. Why girls wore dresses instead of trousers. What was in the box on the top shelf of our parents' wardrobe. Where babies came from. Although we had much in common – like me she wore National Health specs and neither of us was clever – her raison d'être wasn't the same as mine.

Within a short time after we had settled into Gloucester Terrace my sister knew where things were and what they were for. She knew where the keys were hidden to the doors our parents kept locked and what was in the boxes in my mother's dressing table. She instinctively understood when a thing was forbidden and that it was only by taking possession of such knowledge that a child became an adult. She wasn't interested in the sort of things a normal person was interested in: motor cars, ball games, comics, Compton's bowling figures, how to flip a coin with your thumb and catch it – whereas my brother and I weren't interested in anything else.

The reason girls wore dresses, I came to understand, was in order for them to pee squatting down. Until my sister gave me a demonstration of what she was talking about I hadn't known that girls peed any differently to how I or my brother peed, standing up – or even that they didn't have a tossel. When we made a close inspection of each other's pee-ers, she was impressed by the moveable parts of mine, especially the way she could make the foreskin slide up and down over the end of it. She pointed out to me that our dad's tossel didn't have one of these, something I really ought to have noticed myself. Her own pee-er – you could hardly call it a tossel – which I examined with the aid of a torch and Dad's magnifying glass, was a much less interesting thing. There didn't seem to be a lot to it.

But that was where I was wrong. I was learning that there was much more to everything than I had supposed. While my brother collected *facts*, it was *meanings* that my sister was interested in. Looked at through her eyes, the most banal object acquired significance. The drawers we unlocked and rifled contained a jumble of stuff of passing interest to me: scent bottles, old letters in envelopes, postcards of places and photographs of people I didn't know, a book of matches with the image of a grenadier guardsman on the flap, lipstick containers, Coty powder, silver money. Out of this miscellany my sister conjured mysterious items: a round yellow rubbery plug-thing you could turn inside out whose precise function my sister was uncertain of; a black Bakelite tube with a nozzle at one end and a rubber bladder at the other which, she claimed, our mother used to wash out her pee-er. She had seen her do this with her own eyes.

I didn't care a great deal about these discoveries and they meant little to me. But my sister cared. For her they were clues in the story she was piecing together, one that would make sense of her genesis, how she came to be the person she was. This was the purpose of her investigations: to understand the mystery of men and women – or, at least, of her mum and dad. She picked through the bits and pieces in the drawers, sifting the information like an archaeologist. Her apprentice, I was anxious in case Mum and Dad came home and caught us snooping and gave us both a good hiding.

While they were out of the house, in the pub, we explored the out-of-bounds areas of our parents' bedroom. We went through our dad's pockets. My sister made a close examination of the contents of our mum's underwear drawers, of her brassieres, knickers and suspender-belts and nylons. With the hidden key she opened the door to the wardrobe, although even standing on a chair she wasn't able to reach the top shelf.

'Let's fetch the ladder,' she said.

It took both of us to carry Dad's wooden stepladder and set it up against the open wardrobe. While mum's dresses hanging on the rail exhaled her fragrance that I loved so much, my sister climbed the ladder until she stood on the top step. I stood lower down, holding the ladder, watching her. The top shelf was packed with leather suitcases, hatboxes and cardboard containers all jammed up against each other so that nothing could be withdrawn without displacing some other object. While I hoped we wouldn't be caught in the act, my sister patiently handed down Mum's bag of unused knitting wool. Then she wiggled loose from the back of the shelf a pink cake tin, which she passed down for me to take. She followed me down, carrying a square wooden box.

The plain, featureless box she was holding had no back or front or top or bottom, nor any opening, because the six square sections of ply-wood had been nailed shut. There was no question of looking inside the box unless you happened to have a cold chisel and a claw hammer handy. She took the pink cake tin from me and placed the box in my hands.

'Take it,' she told me.

The box was heavier than it looked. As an object, it didn't look very exciting, not after all the trouble involved in getting hold of it.

'Shake it!'

I did as I was told and the contents rasped against themselves: too heavy for wood shavings, not heavy enough for rusty old nails.

'Do you know what it is?' I asked her.

'Of course I do.'

'What is it, then?'

'Hold on. You'll find out in a minute.'

She took back the box and placed it on the floor and then sat on it with her legs apart so I could see her white cotton knickers. She opened the pink cake tin that contained a mass of old documents, Wartime ration cards, identity cards, birth certificates, letters and dusty black and white photographs. She handed items to me to look at.

'This is of Dad as a baby. "May 1903. *The Pirn*". He's sitting on his mother's knee – with his brothers, Duncan and Ian, and his sisters, Margaret and Mary . . .'

'. . . That hill on the other side of the garden wall is Pirn Crag.'

Pirn was my sister's middle name.

She pointed to each of the children and the baby on the woman's lap, naming them for me. It was hard to believe that the smiling baby in the frock and frilly hat was our dad, that the little nose and the littler toes belonged to him whose nose and toes could not be called little.

'Where's our dad's dada?' I ask her.

'He's holding the camera, I suppose. He was dead by the time our dad could walk.'

She took this photograph from me and handed me another.

'. . . And this is Dad in his midshipman uniform. 1919, it says, so he's seventeen years old . . .

‘And here he’s older. “Disembarking from HMS *Magpie*, Feb., 1944”. He’s forty-one. That’s him with the beard . . .’

‘And this is his ship, HMS *Magpie* . . .’

There were photographs of Mum with two girls and an older woman: our aunts, Vera and Isabel, and our grandmother, Lily. I had never seen any of them before.

‘I didn’t even know I had aunties, let alone a granny.’

‘Well, you’ve got two.’

‘Aunties?’

‘Grannies. You have four aunties.’

‘Where are they?’

‘Two in Liverpool, two in Edinburgh. They’ve never met each other. It was Aunt Mary Mum and me lived with in Traquair.’

She handed me a photograph the colour of a Manila envelope. Two children were at a picnic, a boy in a sailor-suit and a pretty girl in a white knee-length dress and black stockings, her hair loose about her shoulders. She was watching him smirk into the camera.

‘That’s our dad. He’s ten years old. And that’s Enid Ballantine. She’s nine.’

'How do you know?'

'It says so on the back.'

'Who's Enid Ballantine?'

'I don't know.'

What she meant was: I don't know *yet*.

She extracted a yellow newspaper page which she carefully unfolded.

'This is the *Tunbridge Wells Advertiser*, she said, pointing to the newspaper title. 'It's for Saturday, 31st August 1946. That's after I was born and before you were.'

She read aloud the column from the newspaper.

INQUEST ON A CHILD

A verdict of Accidental Death was returned by the Coroner (Mr J. H. Soady) at the Kent and Sussex Hospital on Friday at an inquest on Susan Grant, aged two, who had drowned the previous Wednesday after falling into a water-filled car inspection pit in a disused Army hut.

The child was stated by her mother, Mrs Joan Grant, wife of William Duncan Grant, schoolmaster, to have gone out from the former Army hut in the grounds of Holmewood School, Langton village, in which they were living, to play with her four-year-old brother. About half an hour later, the boy came back and asked where his sister was. Mrs Grant, who had been looking after her one-year-old baby, had thought they were together. She went out at once to look for her daughter but could not find her in her usual places of play. She enlisted help and eventually the child was found.

Lewis Greenwood, a member of the school's outside staff, said he found the child's body in the pit of a disused Army hut which was filled with water. Mrs Grant herself pulled the body of her daughter out of the water in his presence but the child showed no signs of life.

Dr Roy Aylward, of Langton Ridge, Langton Green, said that when he saw the child she was dead. She had died quite recently and the signs were consistent with death by drowning.

P-Sgt R. N. Brooker, of Southborough, said the place was the site of what had been a military garage. In the concrete floor, there was an inspection pit six feet long, three feet wide and four feet deep. He said he had examined the scene of the tragedy, and had found that the pit was filled to the brim with surface water from the recent rains.

Difficult to distinguish

'I noticed when I went in that even at that distance you could hardly distinguish which was floor and which was water,' he added.

The actual hut, which until recently had been locked, had been removed, leaving the site open.

The Coroner: Why had the hut been removed?

Witness: It had been sold to a firm and they had taken it away, leaving only the floor, which had flooded with three feet of water.

The Coroner: Why hadn't the firm taken away the floor?

Witness: The firm hadn't been sold the floor.

Finding that death was due to drowning, the Coroner said the mother had been alone in a remote area with three children under five. Susan, while at play, had wandered into what had been a hut and which at that time was unfortunately open of access, and quite unknowingly had stepped into the pit which was then full of water.

'It is one of the most sad and unfortunate things that could happen,' he said. 'The only possible verdict in the circumstances is one of accidental death.'

After my sister had finished reading from the newspaper cutting, she folded it up carefully and replaced it in the pink cake tin.

'Do you understand what it says?'

'No.'

'It says our sister Susan was drowned.'

'But we haven't got a sister Susan.'

'That's because she drowned, silly! Here's a picture of her, if you don't believe me.'

She handed me a photograph of a chubby baby girl who could just stand, a boy's hand clasping her chubby arm, in case she fell over.

'That Mrs Joan Grant in the newspaper was our mum.'

'Joan isn't our mum's name.'

'Yes, it is. It's her real name. Dad never liked the name Joan so he calls her June. She's the one in the newspaper whose baby drowns.'

'How did she drown?'

'Weren't you listening? She fell into a pit in an army hut that was full of rainwater. She was two years old. I was just a baby. Mum was feeding me when it happened.'

A pit. The army. The police. I didn't know what to make of this story. My sister stood up, lifted up the wooden box and laid it in my arms again.

'These are her ashes.'

I knew what ashes were. They were the white cokey bits in the fireplace grate Mum shovelled into a bucket and took out after she had lit the fire in the morning.

'Why is she ashes?'

'Because when a person dies, the body is burned.'

Of all the news I had received lately this was the most startling.

In the box I was holding were the ashes of Susan, my sister. There was a Susan in my class at school. At the time and for ever after, whenever I thought of Susan my sister whose ashes were in the box, the girl I saw in my mind's eye was Susan Elliot in my class at St Mary Abbots School.

'How can she be my sister if I wasn't born yet?'

My sister didn't reply. She returned the photographs to the cake tin – except one, which she passed over to me: a lovely young woman sitting on a step smoking a cigarette was smiling at me.

'This is Mummy in 1947. So she's twenty-five. She looks happy, doesn't she?'

'Yes.'

'That's because she's carrying you.'

'No she isn't.'

She was talking rubbish. I wasn't even in the photograph!

She's *pregnant* with you. You're *inside* her.'

"Inside her what?'

'Her tummy, of course. Didn't you know you came out of Mummy's tummy?'

This sounded like a trick question. My brother and sister sometimes told me fibs, things that weren't true. They liked to see who could get me to believe the most stupid piece of nonsense. Was this one of those times?

After relieving me of the box, she climbed the stepladder and pushed it to the back of the top shelf, and then the pink cake tin. Then she replaced at the front of the shelf Mum's bag of knitting wool I had passed up to her, where she had found it. She descended the ladder, closed and locked the wardrobe and replaced the key in Mum's jewellery box in her dressing table. Together we carried the stepladder back to Dad's work room. She returned Mum's bedroom to how she knew Mum liked it.

'You should be glad she died,' she said.

'Why should I?'

'Because if Susan hadn't died, *you* wouldn't be here.'

'Yes I would.'

'No you wouldn't. Susan died in 1946. You were born in 1947. Mum had you to help her get over losing her baby daughter. If Susan hadn't walked into the water and drowned, you wouldn't be here. So it's a good thing she did, isn't it?'

'Yes.'

Stupid

The move from the garage to Gloucester Terrace was not a great distance, a matter of a single street, but overnight I had to adjust to a completely different set of circumstances. I was no longer free to come and go as I pleased, dress as the whim took me, eat what I could lay my hands on. With the arrival of my mother, the rules changed – or, rather, rules appeared where previously there had been none. I ceased to be a semi-feral scavenger and became respectable. We sat down around a table and ate cooked meals with a pudding. My clothes – those that hadn't been given to Mr McCoy, the rag-and-bone man – were not only clean, they were darned and ironed. Where before I had swaggered and stalked, armed to the teeth, cocksure of my prowess, now I was led, face washed, nails cut, hair combed. If I went out of the house now it was in the company and under the supervision of Mum or my brother or sister. My career as a Noble Savage was over.

On Saturday afternoons I accompanied Mum to one of the parish halls between Bayswater and Portobello where we waited near the front of the queue with the other women for the arched doors to open. If you weren't near the front of the queue, you might as well have not bothered. As likely as not the clothes I was standing up in had originally come from here or somewhere like it, but the main reason we frequented jumble sales was because Mum enjoyed them. She kept her eyes peeled for good-quality women's clothes, swanky frocks, pieces of jewellery, as well as useful gadgets for the kitchen. It gave her a kick to come away with bargains: a pair of Clarks sandals my sister's size, hardly ever worn; a Clarice Cliff teapot; a real fur stole. The dotty posh Christian women who manned the stalls had no idea of the value of what they were selling. But you had to be quick and have sharp elbows. After half an hour of rummaging alongside stout working-class Paddington women – and sometimes men, who were called *dealers* – Mum was all in and withdrew from the fray for a cup of tea and a cigarette. With the coppers she had given me to spend I became the owner of fabulous treasures: a tied bundle of mixed comics; two shiny green tropical beetles (deceased) in a pill box; a 00-gauge Hornby goods van; a 78 rpm record of Mr Charles Penrose impersonating The Laughing Policeman.

One Sunday morning, more out of habit than open defiance, I slipped out of the house and trotted up to the corner where Gloucester Terrace met Bayswater Road, like a dumb animal that follows its nose home. I said hello to my friends Alf and his wife Dot, who gave me an apple and saw me safely across at the traffic lights into Kensington Gardens. Because it was the weekend and sunny, people were out walking their dogs and playing with their children. Winter was over. The fountains were shooting jets of water into the air and fine rainbows of spray blew into my face as I walked between the basins that were now full of water, resenting the presence of all these johnny-come-latelies. I half-expected to run into my old friend Lucy but I wasn't crestfallen when I didn't. A new kind of sadness had replaced the confusion I had experienced following her absence from my life: the knowledge that something final had taken place. I was no longer sad because love had ended but, a harder lesson, because I had come to accept that it had.

I didn't particularly feel like playing on my own – perhaps I had lost that knack too – and so I took refuge inside the hollow oak tree down the slope from Princess Caroline's Temple, squeezing through the gap that was just wide enough for a skinny boy, what my mum called her fourpenny ha'penny rabbit. It was reassuring to see the biscuit wrappers and silver paper on the ground, debris from my previous visits. While I was here, nobody knew where I was. I was in a blind spot in the universe, where I was unknown.

Occasionally, couples or other children passed close to my hiding place without knowing that they were being watched and overheard. The entrance hole framed brief, meaningless snatches of dialogue:

. . . But you said you would!

Did I . . . ?

I watched a tall boy in long trousers looking to right and left between the Serpentine and the fenced-off bushy area. He was looking for someone, calling out a name. The boy knew I was somewhere in the park because Mr Alf's Dot would have told him I was. If I hadn't been so pleased to see him, flattered to have been missed; if I had stayed where I was, hidden in the safest of places; if I hadn't broken cover and run into the open and called his name, as I did do; if I hadn't betrayed myself to him, I would never have betrayed myself to the Invisible Forces of Darkness, and then none of the things that later happened would have happened.

My brother caught hold of me and marched me back by my shirt collar. He wasn't cross with me so much as baffled. He couldn't understand what on earth I thought I was playing at, to be out alone in the park – and, of course, I wasn't able to tell him. He was puzzled that a boy could be so stupid. It would never have occurred to him – why should it? – that I might have a point of view. Being so sensible and clever himself, it was a struggle for him to put himself in the shoes of a person as stupid as I obviously was. It was easier for me to appear stupider than I was than to attempt to express the true nature of my emotions. I didn't have the means to explain to him that I was in a state of mourning, or even to explain it to myself. But if I was stupid, I couldn't be held entirely responsible for my actions. Thus began his perception of me, and my own perception of myself, as a bit of a thickie, a scruffy, boss-eyed, somewhat immature, easy-going half-wit.

Walking back towards the Italian fountains we ran into Dad, who had sent my brother on ahead of him to look for me.

'Oh, there you are!'

Dad wasn't cross with me except insofar as the organising of a search party had interfered with his own plans. All the same, my brother kept me out of Dad's reach in case he thought a thick ear was required. With Dad, you could never tell. On this occasion he couldn't see what all the fuss was about. He knew I had been roaming the park on my own for months without coming a cropper. If anything, he probably felt vindicated that the timorousness of my mum and my brother had proved unjustified. It was typical of Dad's unpredictable nature. Just when you might have expected him to shout blue murder, he was in high spirits.

He suggested, now we were there, that we take a walk around the Serpentine. My brother produced a cricket ball from his pocket and the three of us practised throwing and catching. I was thrilled. I had never played a ball game with my father and brother before. We were all in a good mood now. As we were passing the boathouse on the Hyde Park side of the Long Water, where narrow wooden rowing boats were moored alongside each other against the plank jetty, Dad suggested we hire one and take it out. We thought it would be a terrific idea and so Dad paid the man and we all climbed into the next boat in line, my brother and I facing Dad who effortlessly sculled away from the jetty and steered us around the island towards open water. Dad managed the oars beautifully. Once we had rounded the island he suggested to my brother that he might like to take them, which, of course, he did. Whatever our dad was good at, my brother strove to be good at too, if not better. They changed places – the boat rocking from side to side as they did – and Dad sat down next to me. Dad instructed my brother what to do but, of course, he already knew.

'Did you learn to row in the Navy?' my brother asked him.

'Rowing. Handling dinghies. Sailing. Getting the hang of how small boats behave in water. In review, a midshipman had to be able to stand to attention on the bow-bench of his whaler while his crew rowed in good time without tossing him into the drink.'

'How old were you?'

'When I joined? Thirteen.'

'And when you left?'

'Nineteen. I persuaded Mother to withdraw me and I signed off in January 1921. I was glad enough to swallow the anchor, I can tell you. I hated the bloody Navy. I wanted to have some fun but Mother – or Mother's lawyer, Mr Watt – wouldn't let me have any money. I couldn't do anything about it. I was still a year and a bit shy of my majority, at which I was due to inherit a tranche of Dada's money. The lion's share I wouldn't come into until I was twenty-five.'

'Your father was dead, then?'

'Lord, yes. Long dead. My dada died in 1904, when I was two years old. I called him Dada because my brothers did. I never knew him. He caught a chill visiting a parishioner and died of pneumonia. He was forty-four. Instead of a father I had Mr Watt, the Edinburgh lawyer who had been handling Mother's affairs since Dada had died, and Miss Blacker, her *companion*. I hated both of them.

'Well, to cool my heels, I was packed off to Canada like a character in a Robert Louis Stevenson novel, no doubt in the expectation that I would be eaten by a bear. My sister Mary was already in Alberta, up near the Arctic Circle, doctoring the locals, white folks and natives. She was a tough one, Mary. She was living alone on Peace River in a wooden house in the back of beyond, snowed-in six months of the year. She was completely fearless. She had been one of only two female medical students at St Andrews – and during the War a member of the Scottish Women Doctors Legation to our gallant allies, the Serbs. I was terrified of her. She was the only member of my family I was ever prepared to listen to. As soon as I turned up on her doorstep, she gave me some money and sent me packing, told me she didn't want to see me until the fall, when she had signed me up on an engineering course at the University of Toronto. I was to get lost, in other words.

'Nineteen twenty-two – the year, incidentally, your mother was born – I spent working my way round British Columbia. What a godforsaken bloody place it was! If you've read your Jack London you'll have a pretty good idea about what life was like up there.'

'I've read *The Call of the Wild*,' my brother said.

'Right. Well, there you have it. Primitive little wood-shack towns, hardly any roads, few women, some Indians. Mile upon mile of virgin forest under snow. Eventually I got a job as a kitchen hand to the cook for a railway gang re-laying sections of the CNR track between Prince Rupert and Prince George, above the Fraser River. Luckily for me most of the men were Scots, who looked out for me. It was rough and it was tough, an eye-opener for a boy like me who had spent his life either being waited on in drawing rooms or else battened down under Navy discipline.

'Well, I was in the cookhouse one afternoon, peeling potatoes for the evening meal by the light of an oil-lamp – it got dark by four o'clock, even at that time of year – when a face poked around the tent flap.

'"Would this be Master Luke from the Pirn?"

'I looked over towards the grizzled old so-and-so who was grinning at me.

'"D'ye no remember me?" the man said.

'Well, I didn't. I could tell from his voice he was a Scot, but every second man in that part of the world was a Scot. I had never seen the fellow before in my life.

'"I'm George, Toshie's son. Ye'll remember Toshie, to be sure."

'Well, of course I remembered Toshie. She had been my wet nurse and nanny – a dear, dear woman. I loved Toshie – much more than I ever loved Mother, if the truth were known. Toshie had cared for me as if I had been her *ain bairn*. And here – in the back of beyond, on the other side of the world – *was* her *ain bairn*, George Mackintosh, at one time employed at the Pirn in some capacity or other. As wee babbies we had both pulled on the same tittie. Like a lot of poor Scots, George had emigrated to Canada before the War, looking for a better life, one where he didn't have to doff his cap to his so-called betters.

'After I met George, my lot improved overnight. I was taken up by his comrades – a hard-bitten, whisky-drinking bunch of lowland Scots, several of whom had fought in France. Those fellows were tough, loyal and – sober – gentle as lambs. I joined his gang – on higher wages – and worked alongside them, insofar as I was able. The gang was paid piece work so I had to pull my weight. It was backbreaking bloody work, the hardest manual labour I ever did in my life. They pulled my leg when I spoke from the drawing room or the quarterdeck but George made sure they didn't pull it off. The experience opened my eyes, I can tell you. It was an education.

'George and I quit the gang together at Smithers and, after a few days in the bars, headed for Fort Rupert. You didn't buy a ticket then, not if you could help it. You bummed a ride on the freight trains transporting timber to the coast, jumping aboard on the edge of town, jumping off before the next. It was summer, so you could do this easily enough. But railway guards, who were called brakies, patrolled the trains, and they carried clubs.

'We had covered half the distance. At some wee town George Mackintosh and I were running for a west-bound train. You had to sprint to reach at least the same speed as the train before you could jump on board. I was a fit young man then – I had just completed two years of active service – so I got aboard all right, but George, who was ten years older than me if he was a day, was struggling to make it onto the next car back. I watched a railway brakie on the rear car club the man. I saw George go down. I never saw him again. I never found out what became of him.'

My brother leaned on his oars. We had passed from the Long Water and under the bridge and were lying to in the neck of the Serpentine where the reeds were thick and moorhens nested. A linked chain looped across the water in front of us on which a sign read:

DO NOT ROW BEYOND THIS POINT

– so, of course, he didn't. In the distance, above the raised stone balustrade, the fountains plumed in the Italian Garden. We both waited, wondering if that was the end of the story – or was there more to come? With Dad's stories, there was nearly always more to come.

'After nightfall, as the train rocked down the gradient to the Pacific, I saw the brakie making his way to the front of the train, probably to have a bite to eat and a smoke. He was a big man. He was walking the length of the cut pines and then, when he reached the end, jumping from one car to the next, which is more difficult to pull off than you might think. I could see him coming towards me by his lamp which was flashing ahead of him. I waited between two loaded flat-tops for him to come level and jump and, as he did, I grabbed his leg and pitched the bugger into the spruces edging the track above the Skeena River.'

My brother – facing us in the boat – looked at my dad, appalled.

'*You killed him?*'

'I didn't know if I had killed him. I hoped so. Dead men tell no tales. If he was dead, it could have been an accident of his own causing. He could have missed his footing in the dark. Open and shut case. If he wasn't, well, questions would be asked. But it was a bloody stupid thing for me to have done. I was lucky to get away with it. I've done some stupid things in my life but that was one of the stupidest.

'I stayed on the train, which didn't stop until it reached

Prince Rupert. As soon as I arrived there I went straight down to the dock and took a pier-head jump onto a ship to Vancouver, sailing the same evening. Within a week I was back on Peace River in Alberta with Mary, my heart still thumping in my chest. I stayed put until September. Then I left for Toronto to start an engineering degree at the university.'

Types

Mr Alf, whose fruit and flower stall was next to the entrance of Lancaster Gate Tube station to catch commuters and shoppers, saw me across to the Kensington Gardens side of Bayswater Road and, until Mum arrived, had been my principal source of vitamin C. Alf was one of the network of people who had kept an eye on me while Dad was at his drawing board, working on the contract he was being paid for or on his own account. At night Alf stored his barrow in one of the stables in our mews, four premises along from the garage, so we were neighbours. We shared the same spiv landlord. Like Dad, Alf drank in the V&A, although not in the same bar. Dad sent drinks across the public–private divide to Alf and Dot on the other side. After we had moved up the road to Gloucester Terrace we continued to see Alf and Dot, to say hello to them and, in my case, accept an apple or some grapes from them.

Alf was a *cockney type*. Dad, in spite of his charm, which he could turn on and off like a wireless set, often managed to rub people up the wrong way, especially people in pubs, but he tended to get on well with *types*. Members of Dad's crowd chose to refer to individuals according to their *type*. You might hear one of them say *I was talking to this RAF type . . .* They were happy to pigeon-hole other people and each other according to their occupation or social position. Dad was an

RN type. Gordon Ansell and Yorkie were *army types*.

Of course, none of Dad's crowd was really a *type*. Quite the reverse; they were all non-standard issue. Alexei was a Swiss actor. Yorkie had only one leg. Begbie, the poet. Gordon Ansell, a gentle giant. It wasn't that Dad particularly delighted in the farouche. He didn't choose his friends because they were misfits or unusual but because he suffered from a kind of social astigmatism, which was to avoid at all costs the common-or-garden, the dutiful, the provincial, the provident. He had a horror of sensible people who lived ordinary, blameless nine-to-five lives: bank managers, headmasters, estate agents, inspectors of taxes, stock brokers, magistrates. *Daily Express types*.

One of the *types* Dad got on best with were street-traders, costermongers like Alf – and hawkers like Mr Szymynski, the Pole who sat on the corner of the mews replacing the rattan seats of chairs. Dad and the rag-and-bone man, Mr McCoy, an Irishman, shared an interest in any sort of metal or machinery: electric fires, copper and lead piping. They had a lively exchange economy going between the two of them. When Dad noticed a bomb site that had something of interest to Mr McCoy – lead guttering, say, or ironwork – he received something in return, on one occasion a Bush television set. The television set, which produced sound but no picture, sat in the garage all the time I was there. Dad couldn't do anything with it. Eventually Mr McCoy took it away. After we moved into number 36a, it was Mr McCoy who found most of our furniture: bedsteads, an iron mangle to help Mum wring out the washing, a shirt press to press Dad's shirts, a Singer sewing machine to mend them. They were all useful labour-saving appliances, Dad claimed, and he had got hold of them all cheap. Mum – it didn't cost her a penny to walk around

Whiteley's department store in Queensway – knew that it was stuff someone else had thrown away. She looked at it cluttering up her house and pursed her lip.

On the occasion Dad caught sight of an onion-seller cycling down Gloucester Terrace he hailed him in French, purchased several strings of pink Roscoff onions – far more than we needed and, in Mum's opinion, at an unnecessary extra cost when English ones would do just as well in a Lancashire hot-pot – then invited him back to the flat and sat him down, sent my brother out for a bottle of claret from the off-licence, and the two of them drank and smoked and nattered to each other in the man's own lingo while Mum, rolling pastry with a milk bottle on the kitchen table, flour in her hair, bit her tongue at the shocking waste of money.

'There's one born every minute,' she muttered under her breath. Embroidered on my mum's heart was the motto: *Charity Begins At Home.*

While Dad never worried that the basic necessities would run out – money, food, places to live, credit – Mum did. All she had to spend was the cash he gave her, what was left after he had paid for his car, his drinks in the pub, his swank. If things carried on the way they were going, she told us, we were going to end up in the workhouse.

'Where's the Work House?'

'Number 1, Queer Street.'

Mum – whose own mum's mum had been born in 1868 – lived in dread of the workhouse.

'Steady the Buffs!' she warned me if I reached for a too generous helping of what was on the table. 'We've another day to live, you know. After the feast comes the famine!' And if I didn't finish what I had helped myself to it was because my eyes are bigger than my belly!

'You want your bumps feeling,' she told Dad, bravely laughing in his face after the onion-seller had pedalled off, the bottle of claret empty. 'He saw *you* coming!'

And Mum wasn't wrong, because she hadn't been born yesterday.

When the coalman delivered the coal she gave me as many buttons as hundredweights we had ordered. It was my job to sit on the steps and tell off the sacks, one button per sack, he hoisted from the back of his lorry and emptied into the hole in the pavement in front of 36a.

'They'll try it on if they think they can get away with it,' she told me.

Mum and Dad didn't see eye to eye about any of these *types*. Dad tended to take them at face value, whereas she was convinced it was in the nature of street traders to bilk their customers. This was because she had a distrustful nature, he told her, because she herself was a wretched *lower-middle class type*.

One afternoon Mum and I were alone in the flat. She was making ready to put me into the bath and then to get into it with me. Quite often we had a bath together, partly in order to save on hot water, partly because we both liked the way our skin slithered against the other's in the soapy water. On this occasion – the bath had already run – Mum saw that she had run out of shampoo. Slipping her coat over her nightie, leaving me in my underpants, she hurried to the shop in Porchester Road to buy shampoo before the water cooled.

'If the doorbell rings while I'm out,' she said. 'Don't answer it!'

While Mum was out, the doorbell rang.

Standing on the doorstep was a bewhiskered old gentleman

I had never seen before and who, like Dad, had no teeth, with a scar down his right cheek. He was wearing a worn bowler hat and grey woollen fingerless mittens, and his mittened fist was holding a twelve-inch kitchen knife. He looked like Fagin. I had seen Fagin in *Oliver Twist* at the Roxy with Mum, so I knew what he looked like.

'Is your mum in, boy?' he asked me.

'No.'

'Is she coming back soon?'

'Yes.'

He peered over my shoulder, down the length of the brown corridor to the open door of our flat.

''As she got any knives or scissors what she wants sharpening?'

'Yes.'

Leaving the man on the doorstep, I ran to the kitchen, grabbed the carving knife, the bread knife and the scissors and returned to the front door and handed them over to the man.

Out on the street he had a tricycle onto which a grinding stone had been ingeniously attached. He had a number of knives laid out on a square of felt on the pavement ready to grind. I sat on the house steps watching him, enchanted. As he turned a wheel the grinding-stone rotated, which – Dad would have loved this – he doused with water from a hose mechanism connected to a rubber bladder under his arm while, with the other hand, he laid the blade against the whetstone. The scraping of the metal against the stone made a thrillingly shrill keening sound. Sparks flew.

At that moment Mum came running down the street, her mouth open, although whatever sound was coming out of it was drowned out by the shriek of rough and smooth surfaces abrading each other. She took one look at me sitting on the steps in my underpants and her face went white. She almost went to pieces. I told her it was all right, the knife-grinder man was going to sharpen some knives for us. I felt rather pleased with myself for having fixed it all up for her on my own, without anyone's help. I would have preferred her to have been more appreciative of the ingenious water-dousing feature of the man's grinding mechanism, as Dad would have been.

Mum, beside herself with fury, made the man give all her knives and scissors back to her. Then she let fly. She let him have the sharp edge of her tongue so that you could almost see the sparks flying. The old boy gaped at her, a beautiful young woman with her overcoat over her nightie, as she castigated him for taking advantage of a boy.

She pushed me inside and, as soon as the door of the flat was shut behind us, burst into a flood of tears. Frankly, I couldn't see what she was making such a fuss about.

I crept away, thankful it wasn't me she was angry with.

I thought it best not to mention this encounter to anyone in my family, especially not to my dad, and I was sure Mum didn't mention it to anyone in the family, either.

At the Flicks

If Dad's household was one of Her Majesty's ships writ small, we each knew our position in the naval hierarchy, which might change from one hour to the next. We were either all fellow officers sharing claret cup with the captain in the wardroom or shoulder to shoulder under the lash, scrubbing the decks. My brother was first mate, obviously, because he could use a compass and knew where true north was to be found, although he was already casting his eye over the captain's telescope and larger cabin. His loyalty had not yet been put to the test. My sister, who was never more than a swab pressed into service, was expected to work in the galley and keep a tidy berth. I was cabin boy, Jim Hawkins in *Treasure Island*. Dad was Jack Hawkins in *The Cruel Sea*.

But Mum held no rank at all. None existed for her that she was prepared to accept. Mums didn't figure in the Navy's scheme of things. She didn't know how to give orders and she wasn't prepared to take them. This made it difficult for Dad because it meant he couldn't promote or demote her. She could be neither decorated for loyal service nor clapped in irons for insubordination. Our mum wasn't a member of the crew. She was a landlubber who didn't understand the discipline of the quarterdeck, a beautiful important passenger – Olivia de Havilland in *Captain Blood* – who enjoyed certain privileges and yet, oddly, did all the cooking and washing and ironing. Perhaps she was working her passage. Out of the captain's earshot, she sought to subvert our loyalty to HMS *No Nonsense* by playing on our weakness for Eccles cakes, duff puddings, treacle toffee and soft words. While Dad had us under the cosh of Navy discipline, Mum had us eating out of her hand.

From time to time, instead of going to school with my brother and sister, I went to hospital with Mum. I delighted in these excursions because they meant a day spent alone in her company; I didn't have to share her with any rivals. After our appointment in the morning, these outings often involved a visit to a cinema in the afternoon. We either walked to Paddington Green Hospital, just behind the Edgware Road, or took the Tube to the Brompton Hospital in Fulham. Travelling on the Tube was a terrifically exciting adventure in itself: the escalators that would drag you in if you failed to jump off them in time; the doors to the carriages that opened when you pressed the button; the electric rail that would kill you if you touched it. It was thrilling to be near so much danger while at the same time to be holding my mum's hand.

At Paddington Green Hospital I was asked to perform tricks with my eyes similar to those of the old gentleman in Harley Street, except that now, instead of persuading the pink lion into the yellow cage, I had to put the red nose onto the green face of the clown. That was the only difference, and without the inducement of a chocolate grenadier. The hospital insisted I wore my glasses with the patched right lens all the time, even at school, which meant that I couldn't see the blackboard or Miss Blythe's lips, with the result that I found it hard to hear what she was saying. I could only see out of my right eye; my left was pretty useless. This gave me headaches and made me bad-tempered and I coughed more.

At the Brompton Chest Hospital my mum took off her brassiere and had X-rays taken of her chest, and now and then they took one of mine too. At both hospitals we waited for hours, seated on tube-framed canvas chairs along with fifty other people before the doctor saw us. We were called patients but it would have been more accurate, Mum said, if we had been called impatients.

I came to understand that these hospital visits were not solely on account of my wonky eye but had something to do with Mum. She had her own visits and when she made these she liked to have me along to hold her hand. She wasn't well, I knew that. Every morning I listened to her coughing before she got up. Mum suffered from bronchitis and the reason she had not been with Dad and me at the garage was because Dad's sister Mary, who was a doctor in Edinburgh, had insisted she didn't spend another winter in London because of the smogs, which Aunt Mary thought would kill her. After a particularly smoggy period, such as Londoners had just endured, hundreds of people had died. This was one reason, Mum said, why the out-patients department at the Brompton Chest Hospital was bursting at the seams.

I had a niggling cough myself and the doctors thought at first that I might have what Mum had, which is why they took X-rays of my chest too, but I didn't. All I had was a niggling cough.

The specialist Mum saw at the Brompton was a man called Philip Zorab. Although he wore a three-piece suit and a bow-tie, Doctor Zorab wasn't an old gentleman. Even smaller than my mum, with shiny black hair and a big nose that had black hairs coming out of it, he was more like a very friendly gnome.

He let me use his red Biro to draw on a pad while he examined Mum. Biros were a new thing then and this was the first one I had ever seen, let alone used. Even my brother hadn't used one yet. When I reported back to him how they worked, he said *I know*, which puzzled me. I was sure he didn't know. I didn't understand then how hard it was for him, how great a loss of face, to confess his ignorance about any subject. He was like an adult in that respect. Adults hardly ever expressed surprise or wonderment because to do so would be to put themselves in a contingent position with another person, to come off second best. The important thing was to be the first in the know. To receive information from someone else was to be diminished. Adults liked to tell you what was what; they didn't like to be told. Mr Alf and Begbie and Doctor Zorab were different to other adults in this respect. From the way they talked to you, you could tell that they had been children once themselves. Doctor Zorab said things that made us laugh. Mum thought the world of him. I looked forward to her appointments at the Brompton Hospital, probably more than she did. Disappointments, she called them.

After a boiled egg and soldiers for me and a cup of tea and two chocolate biscuits for Mum at the ABC cafeteria, we made our way to the Roxy cinema in Westbourne Grove, cosier than the Odeon. Once the lights had dimmed, as a treat Mum gave me permission to take my patched glasses off to watch the film, since no one could see us. The newsreel showed the new queen launching her new yacht *Britannia*. Then we watched a film about trains in which some Jubilee class locomotives steamed in and out of a station, covering the passengers on the platform in smoke and steam. One of these, a pretty woman in a hat, gets a smut in her eye which a man, also wearing a hat, removes with his handkerchief. 'Its all *right*,' he tells her.

'*I'm a doctor.*' Amid the smoke from the trains arriving and departing, the man and the woman do a lot of talking over cups of tea and then a bit of kissing. At this point in the film I fell asleep on my mum's lap, nuzzling the fragrances of her body. Afterwards, I could tell she had been crying. It was a puzzle to me why she liked going to the flicks as much as she did, when watching them only made her cry.

In *Oliver Twist* Bill Sikes's dog scratches at the door to be let in while Bill is doing Nancy in. In *Stagecoach* the Ringo Kid shoots at the Indians even though he is handcuffed.

Mum especially liked films starring Fred Astaire and Ginger Rogers. In one of these Fred, dancing in a top hat and tails, sings a song called 'Puttin' On The Ritz':

Have you seen the well-to-do,
up and down Park Ave-noo?
On that famous thoroughfare
with their noses in the air,
High hats and Arrow collars,
white spats and lots of dollars,
Spending every dime
for a wonderful time.

In another film three old men are lying in bed asleep with their beards sticking out over the sheet and a man wearing a pointy hat comes in and, without waking them up, cuts off the three beards with one cut from a pair of scissors. It made us laugh so much tears came to our eyes. More than anything in the world I loved to hear my mum laugh. Nothing was better than to laugh at something she was laughing at.

After the film, we hurried along Bishops Bridge Road.

'Home, James!' she said, my hand in hers. 'And don't spare the horses!'

Dad was waiting for us when we got back home but he wasn't at his drawing board. He was pacing the lino in a foul mood, smoking. He threw us a filthy look as soon as we walked through the door. I knew that look and bolted behind the settee. I could tell he had been in the pub all afternoon.

'Where the bloody hell have you been?'

Dad tended to raise his voice when things didn't go to plan.

Mum stood her ground.

'I had a hospital appointment at the Brompton. Then we went to the Roxy.'

'Jesus bloody Christ! Didn't you have anything better to do?'

She wasn't going to feel guilty for going to the cinema, for what he called her dose of sentimental mush. Soon they were at each other's throats, hurling horrid words across the room. I kept out of the way behind the settee, where my car was garaged.

It was unusual to see Dad the worse for wear. He was never a big drinker. He didn't go to the pub to get drunk. He drank half pints of ordinary. I never saw him lay a finger on my mum but he had a filthy temper that could flare up at any time.

Their row didn't last long. After the storm had blown over, calm was restored. Mum put the kettle on and they had a cup of tea. Then it came out: Dad had lost his job. He had been hired by a firm on a monthly retainer to come up with a design for a machine that would change coins, that would give you two shilling pieces and a sixpence, say, in exchange for half a crown. No such machine existed yet and there was a fortune to be made by the person who got one out first. Dad thought he had cracked it and he wanted the firm to knock up a working model to see how it performed. But if he showed his plans to the firm, they would understand how it worked. He was unwilling to turn over his idea to his employers, who would then own the patent. His employers had ordered him to hand over his drawings, which they regarded as their property. It wouldn't be hard to imagine how Dad had reacted. He would burn his bloody drawings before he complied. And so they had fired him.

Dad wasn't worried about losing his job. Something would turn up. It always had. He had been in much worse scrapes in his life than this. But he was angry with himself. Once again he had done what he always did: he had lost his temper, told his employers where they could stick their fucking job, behaved in such a way that he would have to move on and start all over again. Where did that leave his coin-changer? Like all his other inventions, he would have to hawk it round in search of someone prepared to invest money in it. This chain of events was a fault line that ran through his life, so that he was doomed to enact over and over again the same wretched scene.

But Mum was worried. What were we going to do for money – how to buy food, pay rent? Living from hand to mouth, not knowing where the next penny was coming from, moving from one damp flat to another, coughing all night, was getting her down. The way things were going, we were going to end up on Queer Street. This was not what she had bargained for when she had run away from her lower-middle-class family in Liverpool as a seventeen-year-old girl, never to see her father again after she had thrown in her lot with the handsome old charmer in the blazer with his snazzy car. As she would have been the first to tell any other woman in the situation she was in: she had made her bed and now she had to lie in it.

Later that evening, after supper, while my brother was solving his quadratic equations at the kitchen table, I sat on the bed in Mum's bedroom watching her dress up in her prettiest clothes. After her bath, she stepped out of her dressing-gown and slipped her arms into her brassiere, and my sister, on her knees, pressed the tops of her skin-coloured stockings into the fasteners hanging down from the belt under her knickers. She stepped into her best dress, my favourite: the fitted black one that had a squiggly re-embroidered spaghetti pattern on it, which my sister zipped up the back for her. In her high heels, with her make-up on, the curls in her chestnut-coloured hair carefully brushed to keep their bounce, she looked even more beautiful than Jean Arthur in *Shane*. Dad, shaved and with his teeth in, looked dapper in his black evening suit and shiny black shoes. She was about to accompany him, to cheer him up, to the Coconut Grove in Regent Street. They were getting ready to go out in Old Mother Riley, to dance to Edmundo Ros and His Orchestra, to smoke and drink into the small hours, to tell jokes and stories, dressed in their swankiest clothes. To spend their last two bits, puttin' on the Ritz.

The Comet

My brother succeeded in every endeavour he undertook, mastered whatever skill he turned his hand to. There was nothing he could not do. As well as being an adept bowler of off-breaks, he could feather a ball down to fine leg, almost late square-cutting it. He was handsome and well built, with a profile as debonair as that of Denis Compton in the Brylcreem advertisements on the walls of the Tube stations. He was one of life's natural captains who could swim, run and catch balls, name all the monarchs of England since William the Conqueror, tie a double clove-hitch, draw faces, read Ordnance Survey maps upside down and recognise birds from their droppings. He attended the free Sunday afternoon lectures at the Natural History Museum in South Kensington: *Mimicry in British Coleoptera*; *Fossils from the Devonian Period*. In preparation for his camping trip with his Scout troop he painted every match in a box of Swan Vestas with Mum's red nail varnish, as a precaution against damp. He made exquisite models with his hands, because not only was he good at working in all materials, he could do the measuring as well. You would have thought it would have helped having Dad around to consult when a technical problem arose, but the opposite was the case; in any discussion about the best way to proceed, they rarely saw eye to eye and tended to end up arguing the toss. My brother didn't need his dad's help. He built himself a Chinese violin out of an old Romeo y Julieta cigar box and then taught himself to play it. Mechanically minded, artistically inclined, a gallant sportsman, he excelled in all fields. He was an authority on every subject. The height of Everest was 29,028 feet. Len Hutton scored his 364 runs, out of the MCC's total of 903, in 13 hours 17 minutes during the Fifth Test against Australia at the Oval in 1938. A cricket pitch is a chain or 22 yards, which is 66 feet. Everest is therefore 440 cricket pitches high. The RAF Gloster Meteor jet fighter with a flight speed of 597 miles per hour would cover the distance in 3.3 seconds. There never existed for me the possibility of knowing something that my brother did not already know or had thought of first. What I knew about the world had first to pass through his head before it entered mine. As I received his passed-on items of clothing, so I was handed his articles of faith and dog-eared items of information. I fetched the tool he needed for the job in hand, watching, enthralled, while he dismantled the motor of the home-movie projector Mr McCoy had left, and then affixed the turning mechanism to the treadle of an old Singer sewing machine. By rotating the spools of the projector with the treadle he succeeded in projecting onto our bedroom wall a cartoon of Felix the Cat.

But it was in aviation technology that he excelled. He constructed aeroplanes from blueprints out of balsa wood and tissue paper. The wings and fuselage were cut out of wood, glued together and the paper was doped onto the skeleton, one layer over the other. The process of application, drying and reapplication, took hours, days. Then the assemblage needed to be painted and the identification marking transfers added: the RAF roundel, the jagged swastika. We flew his constructions – the propeller rotating by means of a thick elastic band running the length of the model – over the cricket lawn in Holland Park.

Lately, though, he had given up making Spitfires and Messerschmitts. Keeping abreast of the most recent developments in the field, he was building a scale model of the BOAC Stratocruiser, the Comet. This was the world's first jet-powered passenger airliner, a triumph of British engineering, like RMS *Titanic*. We lived with the project laid out on the floor of our bedroom for weeks until the fumes from the dope and enamel paint obliged him to transfer the model to the bathroom floor. By slow degrees the beautiful replica was nearing completion.

Dad had explained to my brother the principles by which jet-propulsion worked, what a marvellously simple invention it was. Although Dad had spent much of his early life at sea, the air was a much more congenial element to him than water. He was more interested in flying-machines than ships.

'. . . We had the Zeppelins over in 1915. That was really exciting. I was at prep school at Westwood House in Maldon in Essex, swotting for my Osborne Entrance. Zeppelins used to follow the Blackwater and the canal – Maldon is just at the source of the Blackwater – until they got to Chelmsford, where they hit the main railway line from Colchester and Harwich. They'd follow these gleaming rail-tracks into north-east London. They used to come in quite low. One silly occasion they either panicked or were aiming to hit the wood stocks of Sadd Brothers, who were timber importers, because they dropped all their bombs – *plonk, plonk, plonk, plonk* – all along the mudflats which – in the moonlight – must have looked just like the tin roofs of factories. All the barges that were lined up on the other side of the estuary saw these bombs dropping into the mud. They didn't even go off.'

'Could you see a Zeppelin in the dark?' my brother asked him, alert for inconsistencies in Dad's narrative.

'Not at all! We only knew it was there because the immense bulk blotted out the Milky Way. And, of course, we could hear the hum of the four engines.

'We did see one go over once because it was lit up by searchlights from a team that had been put on the other side of the Blackwater at Heybridge. We watched it disappear towards Colchester. It had gone – oh, I don't know – about twenty minutes. We were looking towards London to see if the gunfire flashes could be seen, when the whole bloody sky lit up. This was the one brought down at Cuffley by Lieutenant Leefe Robinson. He had dropped bombs on the thing. He got the first air VC for doing that. And they were filled with hydrogen, don't forget. If you were hit, you just went up like that – whoosh! – in one frightful blast. They were brave men who entrusted their lives to such dangerous technology. They had no parachutes.

'We brought down half a dozen in the end before the Germans stopped sending them over. They couldn't afford the losses.

'The air-raids on London, on the other hand, increased. I remember when Mother came down to see me at Osborne in 1917, she had passed through London and she had been very alarmed. It was a sunny June afternoon. She was staying at her club, which was the Ladies' Victoria Club just off Buckingham Palace Road, and everyone had to dash for shelters because a squadron of twenty Gothas was dropping bombs on London – in broad daylight! There was a lot of fuss in Northcliffe's newspapers over that. It was all phooey, of course. The Germans wanted to win the War just as much as we did. If we had been able to build planes big enough to fly to Berlin, we would have done. Londoners, though, were shocked to see these Gothas, which were extraordinary aircraft. Bloody great things for the time and they had cut-back wing tips that made them look very hawk-like, flying at about 2,000 feet over the capital of the British Empire, dropping bombs wherever they damn well pleased. It wasn't the lives that had been lost that angered Northcliffe, it was the bloody cheek of the Hun!'

Dad hadn't adjusted to the move from the garage any better than I had. At first, he didn't make any adjustment at all. As far as he was concerned the new flat was simply a different place in which to carry on doing the sort of things he had been doing in the mews: drawing at his drawing board, tinkering with his bits of machinery, driving about town in Old Mother Riley, cooking porridge how he liked it cooked in the double-boiler. He walked to the V&A in the evening, as he had always done. He tried to invite the Gang back after the pub shut a couple of times but Mum put her foot down and that came to an end. Her views on Dad's friends were not very different from her views on tradesmen: they were scroungers and ne'er-do-wells, pub bores who were laughing up their sleeves at him, taking Dad for a ride – and the pink-gin women were too unspeakable to be spoken about. At weekends she put on her make-up and accompanied him to the pub or a drinking club. Behind his back, she hadn't a good word to say for any of them.

But of all Dad's cronies it was for Begbie she kept her most scathing contempt. He was a piss-artist, a man with no job or money, family or proper home to go to. Whenever Dad brought Begbie back with him for Sunday dinner, she was silent, her lips clamped shut. She resented his sharing the roast and Yorkshire puddings she had spent all morning cooking.

The more he ate, the less of the joint would be left over to be minced up for shepherd's pie on Monday or something mum called *scouse*. Begbie, grateful for a square meal, always ate more than any of us. Dad didn't try to deny that his favourite drinking chum was a worthless sponger. It was obvious he was. And if he was, well, what of it? He wrote beautiful poems, didn't he? Wasn't that a rare enough achievement?

Begbie had yellow fingers where he had held his cigarettes for thirty years, and yellow teeth where he had smoked them. His breath smelt. Whereas Dad farted with shameless vehemence, Begbie let them off with silent, deadly pungency. On those occasions he spent the night on the sofa, too drunk to find his way home, he placed his glasses carefully in one of his shoes before passing out. He slept with his mouth open. I knew this because, as the first person up in the morning, I was nearly always the one to come upon him sprawled across the sofa like a man who had just been shot in the line of duty, except that this corpse was snoring. His feet in knobbly woollen socks, which hung over the arm of the sofa, smelt even worse than his breath. After he woke he usually had the presence of mind to find his glasses and his shoes and shuffle out of the door before Mum found him. It wasn't as if he would be offered breakfast.

And so I was the first person to visit the bathroom on that fateful morning, the first to turn on the light to behold my brother's model BOAC Comet Stratocruiser smashed to smithereens and torn shreds of paper where someone had trampled over it during the night, someone who had mistaken the layout of the bathroom in the dark because he hadn't been wearing his glasses, who didn't know what was where.

The flat was dead quiet. All the occupants except me were in their beds, sleeping in on Sunday morning, still happily unaware of whatever terrible disaster they would read about in the newspapers that morning. My brother's beautiful aerodynamic jet lay in pieces on the bathroom floor, waiting to be discovered. Mum hadn't got up yet to put on the kettle on her way to the bathroom to have a pee. She hadn't even started to cough yet. Begbie was snoring softly on the sofa with his flies undone.

An Expedition

In accordance with Dad's instructions the family submitted itself to his inspection in what he called our Number Ones: best bib and tucker. He himself had on his Navy greatcoat, his term tie with his medals in his pocket to be displayed when the time was appropriate. My brother was in his Scout uniform with full regalia: badges, scarf and woggle, wide-brimmed bush hat and cleft stick for catching snakes with. My sister, in her suede-collared coat, her blonde bob, looked as pretty as a princess. I was in a Grant tartan kilt. My mother, who alone had turned out without any enthusiasm, wore her fur coat and beret and her sourest expression. She had no desire to be part of his expedition but she had no more choice than the rest of us. We had eaten an early supper and now, about the time she would have been thinking about getting me ready for bed, we set out for Paddington station where we took a Bakerloo Line train to Trafalgar Square.

After some conferring between Dad and my brother, we took up our position on a bench in the Mall, about a dozen plane trees down from the entrance to Carlton House. A few other families had the same idea as us. Working-class Londoners were arriving in dribs and drabs, exchanging matey banter about the weather, which was modulating from summery to blustery. For days the weather had been sweltering and then, yesterday, Dad's barometer had plummeted. The evening wasn't very summery at all. The sky was beginning to spit. The mood at first was good-natured but as darkness fell and the temperature dropped people grew quiet and settled down as best they could for a night to be got through.

My brother set up his Primus stove and brewed us each a cup of tea in his billycan, which cheered us up. He had everything we needed in his haversack: tea, milk, Garibaldi biscuits, nail-varnished Swan Vestas. *Be Prepared* was his motto. Leaving him to look after us, Mum and Dad headed towards Haymarket to refill his water bottle, something they would probably only be able to do in a pub. The lamps came on along the Mall as it began to rain, not hard but steadily, which the nap of a kilt, I found, was efficient in blotting up. My sister, who was wearing only a cotton frock under her coat, began to whimper. My brother was torn between his duty to his dad and his anger towards him, his conscience cleft like his stick. My sister and I put our heads down on the wooden bench and went to sleep.

It was still night, still drizzling when I half-woke up. Mum and Dad, who had returned from the pub, were exchanging words in cross, hushed voices. She wanted to go home; he wouldn't hear of it. I fell back into sleep in her arms until we woke up, stiff and hungry. The sun was trying to shine but it wasn't trying very hard. Although the rain was holding off, we were all damp and cold. None of us, not even my brother, had thought to bring waterproofs. He brewed tea and dished out to each of us our biscuit ration. The bench on which we had spent the night was now anchored in a sea of moving bodies. Even at that early hour a large number of people had arrived and were already staking out positions along the Mall where they thought they would get a good view of the proceedings. Our bench, set well back from the kerb, was too far from the front for us to be able to see much. While we had been asleep, Londoners had arrived early on the Tube and grabbed the best positions. The crowd was milling, seething with anticipation. Police constables strolled among us, good-humoured, accepting cups of tea from Thermos flasks, not expecting trouble. All I could see was the back of men's trousers. We could look over the heads of the people in front of us if we stood on tiptoe on the bench, but if we did that the people behind us couldn't see over *our* heads and they barracked us. Dad attempted to rescue the situation but it was too late. We had been caught napping.

'Look here,' he said, addressing the crowd in front of us. 'My family have been here all night!'

'More fool you, mate!'

Laughter.

'Look out – the Navy's here!'

'Bloody Navy!'

'Pipe down!' Dad, who had his medals on, was telling some army bloke in front of him, who had *his* medals on.

'Pipe down yourself!'

The banter was turning nasty.

Mum looked ill. She *was* ill.

The army bloke, who was smaller and younger than Dad but looked more mettlesome, told him to get lost, unless he wanted to make something of it.

'I'll make of it what I choose!' Dad informed him. Having pushed the situation to the brink, he didn't know how to step back from it. It wasn't in his nature.

'Yeah? You and whose army?'

'Don'tcha mean *Navy*,' one of his mates quipped. 'Wouldn't take him in the army.'

'Too old.'

'Copenhagen! Ushant! Nile and Trafalgar!'

'What's that, Admiral?'

'What the Navy thinks of *you*!'

'He's calling you a CUNT, George.'

'Are you calling me a cunt, Admiral?'

'If the cap fits.'

The bloke took a swing at him, so Dad let him have it. The two of them grappled and swapped blows. Dad had the height but the army bloke was more of a scrapper. Women screamed. At the sight of blood on Dad's face my sister and I burst into tears. The fight became a brawl when the bloke's mates piled in, grabbing hold of Dad – perhaps they were trying to restrain him. He was outnumbered, although my brother was doing his bit, whacking the back of Dad's adversary with his snake-catching stick. At this point a policeman turned up and tried to restore order, bellowing at both parties that they should be ashamed of themselves, that they ought to have a bit of respect on such an occasion. Dad, or perhaps one of the other men, must have caught the copper one because he went down. In a flash coppers were all over us. The last I saw of Dad he was being hauled away by a couple of them. They bundled him off into the crowd. People on each side of us began to push forward as soldiers marched past.

Mum had fainted. She was being stretchered over the heads of the crowd by two members of the St John Ambulance Brigade. My brother – his loyalties shattered – had disappeared. My sister and I, looking round, didn't know which way to turn. A regimental pipe band was playing *Lilliburlero* in time to the crump, crump of their boots. Because they were all facing the same direction, cheering the soldiers and the bands, people failed to notice two nippers trying to attract their attention. Then a roar went up. The crowd ebbed. We were squished and squashed as it surged first this way, then that, like a rip tide dragging us with it. I don't know how my sister managed to keep hold of my hand.

Finally escaping this ordered confusion, we emerged behind the crowd where there was room to move about, looking for Mum or Dad, bawling our heads off, until a policewoman noticed us and took us each by the hand. She found Mum lying on a blanket on a stretcher in a St John's ambulance. Her face was white and we thought she was dead. She wasn't dead; she was dead angry. It was a relief to see my brother when he showed up – his uniform askew and without his stick. He took the situation in hand. As soon as Mum had finished her cup of tea and felt strong enough to stand, he led us to where Dad was sitting behind a Black Maria parked by the steps up to Duke of York Place. He and the copper were chatting together about the War, smoking cigarettes like a couple of old friends. Before Dad was allowed to go, a sergeant read him the riot act, told him he was bloody lucky to be let off. No charges were going to be laid because Dad had fought in the War and had obviously been through the rough stuff. Besides, arrests would be unwelcome on such a happy occasion. Dad shook the copper's hand and that was that. He was let go.

As soon as we were back together again, Mum gave him a piece of her mind. She let him have it. He didn't believe in the royal family any more than she did, and she didn't believe in it at all, so what were they doing there? He was a bloody fool. Fighting in the street? She was too angry to cry, like those bitter mornings she said were too cold to snow.

For once, Dad didn't argue with her.

The show was over. The new queen in her gold carriage with her regiments and bands had marched down the Mall. Patches of blue had begun to appear in the sky, almost enough to make a pair of sailor's trousers. We drifted back towards the Tube station with all the other people in a great gaggle.

Nasturtiums

I had been nurturing my nasturtium seed since May, when my teacher, Miss Blythe, had handed it to me – and to all the children in her class – in the small brown envelope inside a terracotta pot.

'Don't forget to water your seed,' she had said. 'But don't water it too often.'

I had planted my seed in the pot, remembering to water it and not to water it too often. Once a week she asked one of us to stand up and report to the rest of the class what stage his or her plant had reached. Had the shoot appeared? Did it have two crinkly leaves on it? Any tiny buds yet? She held up her own plant for us to compare with ours.

Yes, miss! Mine has, miss!

I put my hand up, pleased to have found something at school I could do with my patched-over glasses on. It was something you had to be clever to do.

Don't all shout at once, please. Hands up!

From Miss Blythe, in music-and-movement, we learnt how seeds curled up tight into a ball: *Curl up tight. Tighter!* How roots grow down for their food: *Push down, children!* How their shoots stretch up – *Stretch up now! Higher!* – to gain light from the sun. From the seed came the plant, from the plant the flower, from the flower the seed again. We grew broad beans against blotting paper in glass jam jars so that we could watch the white root climb downwards, the shoot push upwards, the cotyledon opening.

Music-and-movement with Miss Blythe was always exciting. After having run around with our arms waving about like seeds blowing in the wind, we lay quiet on the parquet floor like seeds lying on the surface of the earth. As Miss Blythe walked among us while we lay on the floor, arms stretched out, eyes closed, I opened my eyes and looked up. For a moment I didn't understand what I was looking at. Miss Blythe was standing over me and what I beheld, under the hem of her dress, was the secret world women concealed beneath their clothes: the tops of stockings, the suspenders, the knickers. It was a mystery to me why women and girls, my mum and my sister and Miss Blyth, were so different, so much more complicated than boys and men, my dad and my brother and me.

I kept my terracotta pot containing my nasturtium on the windowsill outside the window of my bedroom, which was at the back of the house, to catch the best of the sun. Mum had bought me my own watering can and gardening kit from Woolworth's. On the balcony at the front of the house, outside the big bay-window, we planted a packet of mixed seeds. Mum, at the same time as encouraging my enthusiasm for gardening, was doing her best to cheer up the crumbling front of the Victorian building from which paint was peeling from the plaster, here and there the plaster flaking from the brick. As soon as I came home from school I ran to the bedroom to see how much my plant had grown since the morning.

It's hard to say exactly at what stage of the project my dad began to take an interest in it and to grow some nasturtiums himself. Fairly early on. Possibly even before the shoot appeared. Quite soon he had a dozen improvised containers of his own next to my pot, some filled with sand, others with bits of cotton wool, others with some kind of shredded foam rubber. He also had an assortment of bottles containing solutions of chemicals dissolved in water. The windowsill, which wasn't very wide, was becoming a bit crowded. And whereas I was a very tidy gardener and always left my tools inside my watering can, Dad left his stuff all over the place.

Dad had decided to carry out an experiment. He had come across an article in *Scientific American* which had predicted that by the end of the century most of the world's population would be eating food grown in factories. Although he didn't claim to know anything about biology or horticulture, Dad had acquired an interest in hydroponics: the science of growing plants without soil. He envisioned a mechanisation of the growing process: a series of homeostatic machines that would sow seeds, feed plants, monitor and harvest acres of tomatoes or leeks in the Sahara desert. He wanted to see for himself whether plants fed nutrients directly would grow as successfully as plants grown naturally in soil.

I had mixed feelings about Dad's involvement in my school project. To begin with, it immediately ceased to be entirely mine. My nasturtium was now the control plant in his experiment. I found it difficult to separate what my dad said was supposed to happen from what my teacher did. My plant, which had a head start, was always more advanced than any of his, some of which did not even germinate. I would have been glad to look after his plants as well as my own but Dad had given me strict instructions not to interfere with them in case I compromised the experiment. He wasn't watering his plants; he was administering a chemical dose to them with a glass pipette. He was confident that his plants would eventually catch up with mine and overtake it – because, temperamentally, he had more faith in mechanical inorganic processes than he did in natural organic ones. This introduced an element of competition into the experiment. I didn't want to compete with Dad, not because I was afraid he would win but that he wouldn't. I was afraid that his disappointment, if he lost, would be greater than mine if *I* did.

Dad was a materialist. As a mathematician and engineer he scorned metaphysical explanations about the world, perhaps because he was the son of an Episcopalian vicar. There was no place in his universe for God. For Dad, there was no ghost in the machine. All things were subject to the laws of cause and effect and the second law of thermodynamics, from vast distant constellations to the tiniest subatomic particles. As above, so below. In the case of living things, the explanation was simply going to be a bit more complicated than it was for the combustion engine. However, in his eagerness to refute non-scientific mumbo jumbo, he tended to underestimate the complexity of the conditions living things require, the importance of their dependence on other living things. He reduced plants to simple reactive objects of chemical agents, airily dispensing with their supportive ecology.

Dad tended to see every problem as an engineering problem, a matter of simple logistics and complicated mathematics. He moved Mum and us kids about the country from one alien culture to another, without taking into consideration our particular needs, the emotional bonds we had made with particular places and particular people. His vast stellar solutions took no account of our tiny, subatomic requirements. According to Miss Blythe living things had roots that went deep and shoots that reached up, whereas Dad saw us, plants and children, rather as more or less complicated machines that required fuel and lubricants and regular maintenance. The only thing to thrive under this regimen was his motor car, which always looked splendid.

By the end of school term, the middle of July, my plant always had two or three beautiful vermilion blooms on it, which cheered my mum up – possibly, by then, it was the only thing that did. Dad's plants, on the other hand, those that grew at all, were etiolated and yellow. None of them ever really looked like flowering, even though, since he had lost his job, he had taken an even greater interest in the economic potential of his experiment. In the end he lost interest in them and turned his attention to something else.

On the day appointed we each brought our nasturtium into school for Miss Blythe to look at and judge. She examined each red or yellow flower and praised each proud owner. To me she smiled her sweet smile. I loved Miss Blythe.

'Well done, Neil! What a lovely plant! Clever boy!'

I hadn't won the prize, which was a beautiful book called *The Wonders of Nature*, although I was awarded a Certificate of Merit. I didn't feel hard done by. Miss Blythe's smile was worth more to me than any silly old book.

The Ashes

My brother's green baize-covered cricket scrapbook had a lever mechanism that permitted additional pages to be added when required. Already three-quarters full, it bulged and needed both hands of a small boy to lift. Under his supervision I was allowed to cut out the photographs from the newspapers but I didn't have the dexterity to apply the gum and align the cuttings onto the page sufficiently accurately for him, who was scrupulous in such matters. As the season progressed the scrapbook grew in size with thrilling black and grey images of men in whites; of the ball sensationally caught at third slip, swept fine to the fine-leg boundary, removing the middle stump behind a startled batsman; of Truman appealing, Evans stumping, Compton 'walking'. Unless you had attended the match in person, these were the only images of the game available – if you didn't count those in your mind's eye that accompanied the radio commentary to the Test matches. This season the Australians were in England and if we wanted the Ashes back we had to beat them; a drawn series wouldn't be good enough.

It had been a changeable summer. Sunny breezy skies had alternated with relentless downpours, on occasion in the course of the same day's play. Generally speaking, this made for uneven wickets favourable to the spin bowler and the heavy humid atmosphere to the seamer – ideal for one such as Alec Bedser opening on the fifth day with the new ball. On a sticky wicket a bowler who was able to turn the ball, such as Jim Laker or Tony Lock, could be devastating. Hitherto, the feature of the first four drawn Tests against the Aussies had been the part played by the weather, rescuing each side from a drubbing more than once. It had saved England from the embarrassment of going into the final Test one or even two down.

It was a measure of the calibre of Australian cricket that, after Bradman's nonpareil 1948 side, which had not lost a single match on the tour, even this sparkling young England side – Hutton, Edrich, May, Compton, Graveney, Bailey, Evans, Laker, Lock, Bedser, Trueman, with Wardle twelfth man – still found it hard to beat a lesser Australian one. There wasn't a great deal between the two teams. But the less one-sided cricket made for a more exciting game. The home crowd had great expectations of their team. Not since 1934 had England been triumphant in an Ashes series, not since 1926 at home.

I served a useful purpose for my brother, providing a foil for his excitement, since it isn't easy to be excited on your own. Even though my grasp of the game was rudimentary, at least he could discuss the state of play with me, since no one else in the household had any interest in it.

In the Fourth Test at Leeds the Australians had been on top from the moment Lindwall had taken Hutton's wicket with his first ball. Only Bailey's stubborn four and a half hours at the crease on the last day for 38 had cheated the Aussies of victory. My brother and I, as soon as we got home from school, sat with our ears glued to the radio, to the gentle non-partisan commentary of John Arlott – and on Saturday practically all day, from the first ball to stumps. He paced the floor, looking grim, glancing now and then at the clock on the mantelpiece. The issue was one of such seriousness that I barely dared address a word to him. It was enough for me to hold my breath when he held his, groan when he groaned and gasp with relief when he did. For the final Fifth Test, which was due to be played a bus ride away across the river at the Oval, there was never any question but that we would be there at seven o'clock to queue and see the entire third day's play. I had never been to a Test match. The prospect of seeing May and Compton and Hutton against the Aussies was almost too exciting to contemplate. What if it rained, as it had done in all the previous matches?

Even though Hutton had lost the toss for the fifth consecutive time, the first day's play went pretty much England's way, Bedser and Truman doing most of the damage. Then, after being 207 for 8, the Australian tail had wagged. They had been allowed to creep up to a quasi-respectable 275 before being all out. By the time we came in from school the number nine, Lindwall of all people, was on his way to 62. We weren't too worried yet. A good showing by England on the second day and we might still be batting on Saturday. It didn't matter if we were still batting or not, it was going to be a marvellous day's cricket. The weather forecast predicted sunny periods and no rain.

After stumps on the first day – at 6.15, bad light preventing Lindwall from scalping Hutton – we sat down to tea and Mum began to talk about me missing school the next day because I had an appointment at Moorfields. I didn't know she had this planned any more than she knew that Hutton and Edrich would be facing Lindwall and Miller. This was annoying but there was no reason I couldn't be back home before stumps and, anyway, my brother and I would be at the Oval on Saturday, all day.

On Friday morning Mum and I took the Tube to Old Street to see the specialist, Mr Trevor-Roper, in Moorfields Ophthalmic Hospital. I was hungry because for some reason Mum had let me leave home without breakfast. I didn't mind taking all my clothes off and getting into bed because the nurses were pretty and tickled me, laughing while they helped me get undressed. It was only when Mum gave me my golly and said she was going to have to say goodbye that it began to dawn on me that something wasn't right. If she was going to leave, when would she be coming back? She would try and come in on Sunday, she said. Sunday? What about Saturday? Lindwall and Miller could still be bowling at May and Compton by Saturday!

I was distraught and angry, not only because I would be missing the third day at the Oval but because I had been tricked.

'I hate you!' I shouted at her. 'I never want to see you again!'

'Darling, please don't say that!' Mum implored.

I refused to let her kiss me goodbye. By turning my back on her, I was pleased to see, I was able to wound her. It gave me bitter satisfaction when she left to know that she was crying too. Apart from any other consideration, at a time such as this I didn't want my golly. I wanted my car.

Later that morning a nurse snipped off the eyelashes of both my eyes so that they felt disagreeably prickly when I closed them, and then she squeezed some thick ointment into them, after which the world became a blur. Mr Trevor-Roper, the specialist, came to see me and he shone his pen-torch into my eyes. I obeyed his instructions and let him do what he wanted. He tried to jolly me up.

'And how's Mr Golly?' he said.

He shone his torch into my golly's eyes.

He was wasting his time. I had lost the will to live, let alone laugh. I was given something that made me drowsy before the anaesthetic. This would have been about the time Evans and Bailey were pulling the coals of the English innings out of the fire.

The principle behind the kind of operation I was about to undergo was that the muscles controlling the shape of the eyes were cut shorter – since it wasn't possible to make them longer – in order for the lenses in front of both eyes to align themselves so that they were able to act together instead of going their own way. That was the theory. The muscles controlling the lazy eye would be altered to compensate for their divergent pull. It was a fairly crude technique done with razor blades and a needle and thread.

When I came round later that day, or perhaps the day after that, I couldn't see anything because my eyes were bandaged and the violence of the pain was as much unexpected as it was disagreeable. I screamed and shouted and struck out at the nurses. I didn't behave well at all. I didn't want to behave well. I wanted to behave badly. In the end a nurse gave me a shot of something that sent me back into the Land of Nod. After a couple of days of this – sleeping, waking from darkness into darkness, strange voices urging me to drink or eat what they were offering me, cross because I refused – my bandages were removed. My gummed up eyelids were teased apart, after which I could see the green-baize blinds pulled down over the windows, reminding me of the cover of my brother's scrapbook and the reason for my misery. Ointment was dropped onto my eyeballs to prevent them drying up, allowing my tears to flow more easily, with the result that everything became even more blurred.

My mum and dad came in to see me but I was too distraught to talk to them. I let Mum hold my hot hand in hers while she murmured comforting words to me. I pretended I wasn't paying attention to her soft words, hoping to make her cry again. I could hear my dad playing with the other children in the ward, dancing them around the floor with their feet on the top of his shoes, something he had never done with me.

When I looked at my mum I saw two women, two blurry faces – although I knew that really there was only one of her. It hurt me to glance sideways too quickly, something it's hard to stop yourself doing. I had to move my whole head slowly in order not to wrench the stitches on either side of my eyes. I didn't understand why my eyes had been operated on and I blamed my mum for letting them do it to me.

I would still have to wear glasses, Mr Trevor-Roper told us, but at least now I wouldn't have to wear a patch over my right eye, the badge of my imbecility. At least I would look like a normal boy. The thing was that now, because my left eye was so weak, I saw two images superimposed on top of each other and it was hard to see either of them clearly. Only if I covered my left eye could I see anything at all. It seemed to me that my eyes were in a worse state than they had been before I had gone through this bloody palaver.

In the end it was Mr Trevor-Roper, during his final visit to shine his torch into my eyes, who passed on the news: we had beaten the Aussies. After nineteen years, we had the Ashes back. I didn't feel as triumphant about our victory as I thought the occasion required.

Queer Street

It rained during the remainder of August, as it had rained most of the summer. With my recently re-engineered binocular vision I watched the traffic through the rain-washed windows, waiting for something to happen. The seeds Mum and I had planted in the window-box in spring had blossomed into yellow ragwort and pink bay willowherb. School had finished and we had nothing to do except knock around the house, getting under each other's feet and on each other's nerves. Dad, who wasn't at his drawing board so much now that he didn't have a deadline to meet, sat in his chair filling in the *Manchester Guardian* crossword, trawling the situations vacant in the engineering trade press, ash from his cigarette dropping from his sleeve onto the floor. When he wasn't at home he was out in Old Mother Riley to promote his ideas, buying drinks for anyone who showed any interest in them. He was able to keep his car on the road because a local garage allowed him to buy petrol on the slate. He couldn't bring himself to get rid of her. It would have been a false economy.

Mum, her hair turbaned like a char's, cleaned the flat, cooked meals, washed clothes, dragged us round the shops in Westbourne Grove. She had her work cut out looking after three kids, making ends meet, keeping Dad sweet. She put a brave face on things for our benefit but she was worried sick about money. She couldn't see how we were going to pay the milkman and the laundry company, the gas and electricity bills, and it cost a fortune to keep Dad in cigarettes and newspapers and pub drinks. She hardly ever went with him to the pub any more. She stayed at home, looking drawn, without make-up, her hair falling across her brow, coughing. She didn't look well. And yet how marvellous it was to stand on a chair next to her at the kitchen table covered in flour, to plunge fingers into the soft dough and then, after she had peeled the Bramleys for the pie, to dip the peel into the white sugar, hold it at arm's length, to lower it into the mouth like a sword-swallower swallowing his sword; to devour the piping hot miniature Eccles cake she had made for me out of the remnants of the batch; to watch the treacle toffee cooling in the tin tray and then to hit it with a hammer and eat the pieces with her.

Dad's solution to his temporary financial difficulties was to open an account at Whiteley's in Queensway, where we could buy anything from a bowler hat to pork sausages and, for Sunday, a leg of lamb and sprouts – much more dearly than Mum could have bought them at local shops but on tick and have them delivered in the Whiteley's van. It would be a month before he would be sent a bill, another month before the bill had to be paid, another month still before his credit was withdrawn. He would have three months before he had to settle up – which would take him to November, and then they would have to take him to court if they wanted to see any of their money. This was the double-entry accounting margin in which Dad thrived. He didn't have to pay with cash until Christmas and by then something would have turned up. Almost certainly.

A man from the gas board called early one morning, just as Mum, who was in her nightdress, was running herself a bath.

A cheerful cockney, he said he was very sorry but he had come to cut off the gas because the bill had not been paid, although he didn't mind waiting until Mum finished running her bath. I followed him down to the cellar, where the gas meter was, next to the coal hole, and held his torch while he closed off the valve and disconnected the meter from the gas pipe and the house pipe. He affixed a lead seal to the meter to prevent us using it until, he explained, we had paid the bill. This meant that Mum, who was in the kitchen with her face in her hands, had no means of cooking or heating water. She couldn't even boil a kettle to make a cup of tea.

As soon as the gasman had left the house and cycled off down the road, Dad showed himself. He was holding a two-foot length of rubber hose from a car radiator-pump. He and I descended to the cellar, where I held the torch for him while he clamped one end of the hose onto the gas pipe and the other onto the house pipe with a couple of hose-clips, by-passing the meter and the lead seal, and then he pulled down the lever that opened the valve. It took him about twenty minutes.

Dad expected Mum to be pleased – not only had the gas supply been reconnected, it had been reconnected at no expense – but she didn't say anything. She just lowered herself into her bath and shut her eyes.

I didn't see much of my brother that summer. Perhaps he was away on Scout camp. I don't know where he was. He returned briefly and then left almost immediately for an interview at a boarding school on the River Orwell in Suffolk. Woolverstone Hall was a grammar school for bright London boys who faced difficulties at home, run by the London County Council. He could study Greek and Latin there, be coached in cricket and rugby, paint in oils, run for his House, just as if he were at a public school. He could watch birds along the river, sail dinghies on the estuary, observe the stars through the school telescope. More importantly from Dad's point of view, he could do all these things for free. In his absence, it was my sister's responsibility to look after me. This didn't mean that we had hiding and chasing adventures in the park, fished for tiddlers in the Round Pond, practised catching a cricket ball. Instead of doing any of these things, we kicked around the flat. I fell into her orbit. My allegiance to my brother didn't waver but with no one to read me the cricket scores, it became harder for me to sustain an eagerness for Middlesex to win the Championship – or was it Surrey?

My sister's adventures were not out in the world, in the park or the street, but closer to home, in the realm of philosophy called ontology: the battle between the vorpal blade of her being and the jabberwock of her nothingness. By looking for answers to a number of small, apparently unimportant questions she sought to arrive at the answer to the one Big Question: who she was to be. There was nothing speculative in her search. She was a sleuth sifting through dull facts, following leads into dead-ends, turning up something now and then. She was patient. The old photograph, the enigmatic telegram, the yellow newspaper cutting, the legal document, whose concealed location throughout the flat she came to know of, would eventually elucidate the mystery of her being and vanquish her nothingness.

She was interested in everything, from the geography of Canada to human biology, but only insofar as the matter touched upon her own quiddity. Her deciphering of the world at large was pursued solely to further her understanding of her own position in it. It held no interest for her in itself. She was driven to seek out the facts of life – how babies were born, where, when and to whom – and when she was in possession of these facts she would know the secret combination to the padlock that secured her to her oar in Dad's galley. It was a single-minded quest which she would stick to until she had picked the lock and was free.

She had discovered that much of the information she sought was to be found in the pages of the *Encyclopaedia Britannica,* not in the printed entries but in documents and scraps of paper that had been slipped into the volumes for safe-keeping. Our dad used the *Britannica* as a rough and ready archive. It was from this source that she learnt – and duly passed the information on to me – that Mum and Dad were not married. My mother had my father's name, my sister explained, not because she had married our dad but because she had *assumed* it instead of using her own name.

'Why can't she use her own name?'

'A woman whose name is different to the name of the father of her children isn't proper. She's improper.'

Information to do with my dad was never as straightforward as it seemed at first sight. My sister read out to me documents that threw light – or, so it seemed to me, shadow – onto our parents' past. These documents meant little to me at the time. Even much later, when they were yellow with age, crumbling between my fingers, they still baffled me:

THE STROLLING PLAYER

Remarkable evidence was given at Exeter Police court today when a young Edinburgh man of private means, formerly a midshipman in the Royal Navy and lately a member of a party of strolling players who have been touring Devonshire, was charged with the theft of an Exeter doctor's car on Tuesday of last week.

At the end of August Mum collapsed in the bathroom. She had been feeling a bit poorly lately and one afternoon she keeled over after some vital organ had ceased functioning. She lay on the floor like a dead person and Dad – scared – ran upstairs to our neighbours, with whom we were generally rather cool, to beseech the use of their telephone. Then, in rapid succession: the ambulance, the stretcher, the red blanket, the doors closing on her like the lid of a coffin, her exit and absence.

For my sister and me it was the beginning of being passed from pillar to post. We spent a period with Violet, whose flat was close by and was splendid beyond anything we had ever seen before – silk sash curtains with pelmets, pouffes covered with the same silky material, wall-to-wall carpets – and there were always delicious things to eat: shop-bought cakes, wrapped chocolates in boxes, bananas. Violet spoiled us rotten. For the first time in our lives we experienced the dull satisfaction of sitting in front of a television screen for several hours at a stretch, often staring stupidly at the test card. During those periods that Dad was not at the hospital we knocked around the flat, at a loose end, bored and frightened. The flat, which was no longer being tidied or cleaned, had begun to look scruffy, a jumble of uncared-for stuff that accurately reflected our own confusion and anguish. It was beginning to look as if Mum was going to die. If she did die, what difference did it make that the table had not been cleared of breakfast things by tea time, that the milk had soured or that the marmalade jar was flyblown?

As well as bronchitis in her lungs, Mum had TB in her kidneys. One of her kidneys had stopped working altogether and it was going to be touch and go whether or not the doctors could save the other one. My sister and I were allowed to visit her once in her own isolation ward in St Mary's Hospital in Praed Street, probably because it was feared it might be our last opportunity to see her before her other kidney packed up. We were given surgical masks to put on. She lay completely still, her head lolled back against her pillow, her face slack and horribly white, her eyes hardly able to focus on us, her mouth was opening and closing slowly. An IV tube passed into her arm from a bottle on a stand. My sister and I, on either side of the bed, held each of her hands, which were already the cold hands of a dead person. In a short time she would be taken to the operating theatre and that would decide her fate one way or the other. Her surgeon was called Mr Scorer.

There are two kinds of TB – a negative kind which is not contagious and a positive kind which is. The first kind is dangerous for the patient, the second for the patient and anybody he or she comes in contact with. Mum had the positive kind. My sister and I spent a lot of time in and out of Paddington Green Hospital on our own account, undergoing X-rays and BCG tests to see if we had contracted the disease too. The doctors found it hard to believe that we hadn't. Secretly we hoped that we had because then we could stay with Mum. If she was going to die, we wanted to die too.

Meanwhile, the fabric of our home life was decaying by the hour. The household had ceased to be one of Her Majesty's capital ships, Dad on the bridge issuing orders; we, the crew at our stations, carrying them out. It had become a squalid raft of survivors from a wreck, drifting rudderless on the open sea. With my brother not present to put order into chaos and stiffen morale, nor Mum on hand to give us heart, our departure from the sinking ship was not going to be an orderly lowering of lifeboats and the Birkenhead Drill but Every Man For Himself, the crew and the crew's belongings slithering pell-mell down an acute angle into the cold wet stuff.

Our brother had visited Mum in hospital and then been packed off early to his boarding school – taking with him his smart new uniform, his bat and pads and box of spare Nettlefolds (of Nottingham) cricket boot studs – and it was nearly two years before we saw him again. Dad, who had been given notice to quit the flat by the landlord for non-payment of rent, was finally beginning to get rattled. At the court hearing, he dragged us in front of the magistrate, who agreed to stay the order for eviction for a week to allow this old Navy man wearing his medals, with two young children in tow, to sort out his affairs. One way or another Dad would have to leave Gloucester Terrace within seven days and in that time find a place for us to live.

Towards our removal to this as yet unknown safe haven the family possessions – books, toys, pots and pans, winter clothing, the iron and the ironing-board, Mum's clothes and things – were packed into cardboard boxes, tea chests and suitcases, and these were stacked at the window end of the front room. Among items that were totally worthless were the few pieces of real or sentimental value: the pink cake tin containing family documents, the *Encyclopaedia Britannica*, Mum's hatboxes, Dad's drawing board and instruments, my brother's stamp collection, his green baize-covered scrapbook of the 1953 cricket season, Mum's jewellery box, some things that had come from Dad's family in Edinburgh and had escaped the pawnbrokers – the silver mustard pot with the blue glass container, the Japanese screen. My nasturtium. The piled-up containers of our property – which could easily have been mistaken for unsorted contributions for a local jumble sale, the provenance of much of the stuff in the first place – stood waiting to be carted off to our new address: the Work House, Number 1, Queer Street.

The square plywood box with the nailed-down sides still nestled among Mum's hatboxes and bags of wool that were now stacked on the bare floorboards. It was still a featureless and eerily pointless object to me. Because I associated *ashes* with the recent titanic contest between us and the mighty Australians, I understood the gravity of the word. The box and what it contained – which in some obscure way, according to my sister, was pertinent to the reason for my being – was going to have to take its chances with all the other bits of stuff and rubbish, like the rest of us, in the maelstrom that was about to strike.

The Strolling Player

From the *Exeter Express & Echo*, Wednesday, 17 July 1927:

THE STROLLING PLAYER

Remarkable evidence was given at Exeter Police court today when a young Edinburgh man of private means, formerly a midshipman in the Royal Navy and lately a member of a party of strolling players who have been touring Devonshire, was charged with the theft of an Exeter doctor's car on Tuesday of last week.

The defendant, who was arrested near Honiton the same afternoon under dramatic circumstances, had taken the car from Southernhay East, he declared, on a sudden impulse – with no intention of stealing it – while exercising his dog. He put his dog in the car, went to St David's Station and collected his luggage and set off for Crowborough in Sussex, where he had a friend he was very anxious to get in touch with at the earliest possible moment.

The accused was William Luke Ferguson of 19 Eglinton Crescent, Edinburgh, and he was charged with stealing from Southernhay East on July 10 a Morris Oxford car, value £200, the property of Percy Dillon Warburton. Ferguson, a tall, clean-shaven man of 25, of slim build, was smartly attired in a navy blue suit. He was represented by Mr Ernest Crosse who pleaded not guilty and asked that the Bench deal with the case summarily.

The Chief Constable outlined the case. Mrs Warburton, he said, had placed her Morris Oxford coupe two-seater outside her house, 15 Southernhay East, at 2.15 on Tuesday 10th and at about 4.20

when she came out again she found it had gone. The Police were notified and they telephoned all stations in the vicinity. PC Squires of the Devon Constabulary received this information and while he was cycling from Honiton to Broadhembury on the Honiton-Cullompton main road he saw the car FJ4191 1½ miles from Honiton and on the brow of the hill overlooking the town. Squires approached the car on foot and when he got near he saw the defendant seated in it, examining some papers. When the prisoner saw the constable he at once put his left hand on the brake lever and tried to release it. The constable sprang onto the running board and, leaning through the window, caught hold of the man but the prisoner pulled himself away, opened the door of the car and ran down the road towards Honiton. Constable Squires gave chase, apprehending him after about fifty yards. Asked if he had taken the car, the accused replied that he had. The constable took him to Honiton in a passing car and then communicated with Exeter police.

In Mrs Warburton's car were found, in the dickie seat, a case and an opened wood box both containing clothing, the personal property of the defendant and there were also the defendant's umbrella, walking stick, golf clubs and Sealyham terrier. When charged the prisoner said: 'I took it' and asked to be allowed to see a solicitor.

The Chief Constable submitted that every circumstance in the case was consistent with larceny. The defence, doubtless, would be that the prisoner did not intend to steal the car, but it was taken twenty miles away conveying the prisoner and the prisoner's belongings.

Mr Crosse submitted that the larceny law laid down specifically that the offender must intend to convert another person's property permanently to his own use.

The Chief Constable submitted that if this sort of defence could be raised when a person was caught with somebody else's property there would be no end of it. That defence would apply if, on a cold day, a man went to a restaurant without an overcoat and took one from the stand and went home with it.

Mrs Warburton gave formal evidence as to the loss of her car and said that in the pockets there were her own and her husband's driving licences and an itinerary of the route to London.

Evidence in support of the Chief Constable's statement was given by Constable Squires, an athletic-looking young man who said he was stationed at Broadhembury.

'How many miles is that from Exeter?' asked the magistrate.

'I'm afraid I could not tell you,' the witness replied. 'But it's about five miles from Honiton to Cullompton.'

Mr Crosse, cross-examining, asked: 'When you went up to Mr Ferguson, did you have any handcuffs in your hands?'

Witness: 'My handcuffs were in my hip pocket.'

'Why didn't you take them out?'

'I could not get at them in time.'

'Didn't he then have a fright and run away?'

'He was frightened when he saw me approach.'

'My instructions are that you did produce the handcuffs.'

'I am on oath, sir, and I say I did not. I put one on him afterwards and held the other myself. Once hit, twice shy.'

(Laughter)

'You did not catch him, did you? He stopped.'

'He was winded.'

'You caught him in fifty yards?'

'I was cycling downhill.'

'You had no trouble with him?'

'Not after he ran away.'

Mr Crosse then put his client in the witness box.

Ferguson, who spoke firmly and in clear-cut tones, said he had been in Devonshire for about six weeks touring with a company of strolling players. The troupe had given a performance in Hartland on July 9th and he had left early on the morning of the 10th because of a letter he had received that made him want to get to Crowborough in Sussex urgently. He declined to say the nature of his business in Crowborough. He had wired from Barnstaple to Crowborough and asked that a reply be telegraphed to him at the New London Hotel in Exeter. While waiting for the telegram he exercised his dog in a pleasure ground. No reply had come by 3.45 and he crossed the street and went to Southernhay.

'And did you take this car?'

'Yes,' replied the witness.

'Why did you take it?'

'Well, I could not get to London and down to Crowborough in time that day by train and I was very worried about what I had heard. I thought the car would get me there quicker.'

'And what had you heard?'

'I would rather not say.'

Ferguson declined to expand upon what was worrying him: it involved a young lady and it was not his intention to have her name mentioned in court.

Under further examination the accused said he had £3 7s 4d in his pockets at the time, which would have been plenty for the railway journey if there had been time. When he took the car he meant to get to Crowborough and as soon as his business was over he wanted to come straight back. He had intended to leave the car in the precincts of Exeter. He meant to communicate with the owner of the car but had not made up his mind how he would do this.

When he took the car he had put in his dog and driven to St David's Station where he collected his luggage. By mistake he left by the Tiverton Road instead of the Taunton Road and so he afterwards crossed from Cullompton to the Honiton Road.

Mr Crosse: 'Why did you stop outside Honiton?'

The witness: 'I had lost my way, quite frankly, and the car was worrying me. I wanted to get to a telephone and find out what the reply to my telegram was. And I was worrying as to how I could get to a railway station, leave the car and go straight to London. I was looking through the car to find out who it belonged to – it struck me I should find out that first – when I was arrested.' The accused further stated that the constable who arrested him had put one hand through the window to prevent him from touching the instrument panel and he produced a pair of handcuffs and said, 'You had better put this on and come along with me.'

'What did you do then?'

'I lost my head and made a dash for it.'

The defendant added that he ran only about the length of a cricket pitch and saw that it was rather fatuous and so he turned and went back to the constable who was just then getting on his bicycle. At Honiton he told the police sergeant that he had taken the car because there was somebody he had to see in Sussex. It was, he had thought at the time, a matter of life and death. He was looking for the name of the owner when he was arrested so that he could return the vehicle. He said it was the sight of the car that had made him decide to take it.

Replying to the Chief Constable, the defendant said he had been at Osborne and Dartmouth Colleges and had left the Navy in 1922.

'By going out by the Tiverton Road you avoided passing through the city.'

'That was not my thought.'

'I suppose if you had kept this car at Crowborough for a couple of months and had in your mind the intention to return it you would still think you had not stolen it.'

'That is not the suggestion I would like.'

Mr Crosse said his client's action had been very foolish and he had been instructed to tender a humble apology to the owner of the car. He could not uphold Ferguson's action in any way but at the same time the defendant had not wished to permanently deprive the owner of the car. As the police knew, a reply had come to the defendant's telegram in the course of the evening and if the defendant had received the reply he would not have set out at all.

Replying to the Bench, the defendant said that since leaving the Navy in 1921 he had been travelling in Canada and France. He had no occupation.

The Magistrate announced that after careful consideration of the case the Bench would decide if there was a case to answer and would remit to Quarter Sessions. Bail was allowed on two sureties of £50.

The defendant was asked to bear in mind that, if found guilty, a custodial sentence was within the Court's powers.

At the Seaside

The first weekend in September was sunny and warm. On the ledge outside my window my nasturtium flower was almost too red to look at, like an open wound. Five minutes away at St Mary's Hospital in Praed Street our mum was waiting to have one of her kidneys removed by Mr Scorer. My brother was in Suffolk at his new boarding school. The cricket season was over and I was glad it was too. Without my brother on hand to give me the facts and interpret them for me I didn't know which county had won the Championship. Without him to define the appropriate emotion for me, it didn't seem to matter a great deal. I looked forward to the close season, which I associated with fog, inanition and fried corned beef sandwiches shared with Begbie. I was looking forward to a return to Kensington Gardens deserted, to drained fountains and pea-soupers; to being on my own in the dead of winter in my balaclava and flying helmet and with my spear, a lone hunter in the snow, the crunch of white grass underfoot. I had no way of knowing that what I was looking forward to had gone for ever.

First thing Saturday morning, because it was such a fine day, Dad announced to me and my sister that he was going to take us to the seaside. Even though this was just the sort of unexpected impromptu gesture it was in his nature to make, we were still taken by surprise. He tossed a few odds and sods into the boot of Old Mother Riley, including, to our delight, two brand-new tin buckets and spades and an uninflated plastic beach ball. We piled into the car, which was soon growling into the traffic in the direction of Notting Hill Gate. I had never been to the seaside before, but I had seen pictures in books of families on the beach throwing beach balls to each other, children paddling, playing in the sand, crab-fishing. I was sure I would know what to do when I was there.

For the first part of the journey I sat in the front next to Dad, vrooming my MG car on my knees while my sister sat behind us, getting ready to be sick. It was a hot, tiring drive and I ended up asleep in the back, my head on her lap. I woke up as we were approaching our destination, after the engine had fallen silent. We were at a level-crossing. I climbed out of the car in order to stand on the bars of the gates and watch a King Alfred class locomotive and fourteen carriages in the green livery of the BR London to Plymouth Express decelerating into Torquay. The fireman, leaning out of the cab with a cigarette between his lips, waved to me. I felt as if I were inside one of the illustrated pages of a Ladybird reading book: *Look! John is standing on the gate. George the fireman is waving to John. John is waving to George. He is going to the seaside.*

Back inside the car, the delicious acrid smell of smoke still in my nostrils, I waited for the white gates to open, for one exhilarating page to be turned onto another. In front of us was the bluest sea it was possible to imagine. We were driving into a town that looked exactly like the pictures of seaside towns I had seen in books at school. Strange narrow streets were crammed with happy, red-faced holidaymakers. We could smell the salt in the sea air and on the fish and chips. Against the distant blue, immobile white spinnakers dotted the bay.

Children are playing on the sand. They are laughing. John is throwing the ball to Janet. Catch the ball, Janet!

Outside a pub, seated behind a low wall above the quayside, my sister and I drank lemonade and ate pasties while Dad refreshed himself at the bar. Stretched below was the crowded beach. Families were running in and out of the blue water, something we would soon be doing ourselves, as if the low wall were a dam holding back the marvellous time we were going to have any minute now. Our sense of anticipation was barely bearable. I only wished our mum and my brother could have been there to share it with us.

We expected, when we got back into the car, that we would drive straight down to the beach. This was the logical thing to do. I was impatient to use my new beach ball and bucket and spade. Instead, Dad drove us a little way out of town, first down and round, then up a steep bluff – the sea began to drop further and further away – until we reached a golf course on the cliff's edge and, unremarkable on the landward side of the road, a big ugly house set back in its own grounds. Dad drew up outside a pair of iron gates. He put the handbrake on, got out and pushed the gates open. He nosed the car through the gates and along a gravel drive that embraced an enormous lawn. At Dad's command my sister and I climbed out and waited while he bundled our stuff out of the boot. He headed towards the house and we followed him, unsure what else to do.

In a quiet, wax-smelling vestibule we stood next to Dad while he conversed with two women who had approached him, both of whom – bizarrely, it seemed to me – were dressed in identical clothes, like twins. Every garment they wore, from their ankle socks to their frocks and woollen cardigans, was the same pale shade of grey – except for the belt on their frocks, which was maroon with a silver clasp.

They were like figures in a black and white photograph, flat and unresponsive. On the front of their frocks they wore a brooch in the shape of a sword, the blade pointing down, the hilt making a cross. Neither of them was wearing lipstick or nail varnish or jewellery like our mum or Violet or Miss Blythe or any women we had ever seen. Neither of them smiled and their flat, unresponsiveness frightened me.

We followed the women into a large hall. In one direction, through broad French windows that ran along the length of the hall, we were able to glimpse the blue of the sea hazing into the horizon, looking further away by the minute. In the opposite direction, through the open door to a small office with a desk in it, Dad, tall in his blazer and cravat, was in conversation with an old lady also dressed in grey, who had grey hair that matched her tunic. From small indications I got the impression that my sister and I were the subject of their conversation. I spun the wheels of my car nervously.

Having concluded their talk, Dad and the old lady emerged from the office and rejoined us. He explained to us that this woman's name was Sister Slater; we were going to be spending the next couple of weeks in this house and she was going to look after us. This was going to be our home for the time being. It looked awfully big to me, just for the two of us. My sister, quicker than me to grasp the significance of the situation, had begun to sob quietly to herself.

Dad glanced at his watch. He was eager to push off back to London. If he put his foot down he might make it to the V&A before last orders. He told us we were to be good children and to do as we were told. He would return and collect us very soon, in a couple of weeks' time at the outside. He shook hands with Sister Slater. He didn't kiss us goodbye or take us in his arms, although we might have been even more alarmed if he had. My sister held my hand as we watched through the French windows our dad walk down the drive, turning to give us a final cheery wave before getting into Old Mother Riley. Then, after slowly reversing the car through the gates, he drove away, out of our lives.

We were alone with the three women dressed in grey. Was it possible they really were all sisters? It didn't seem likely. For a start, they didn't even look like each other. While they conferred among themselves we stood next to our pile of stuff until a much younger woman came along and, crouching down to our level, took us by the hand and asked us our names. Her own name, she said, was Brodie. Although she was dressed identically to the other women, she wasn't anyone's sister and the belt of her tunic was green. We clung to Brodie, who was young and pretty and had a friendly smile, while she showed us around the house. The nursery for the little ones. The playroom for the middle-sized children. The quiet room for the older girls. The bathroom with the row of infant washbasins. The outside cubicles containing toilets. The windowless chapel. I had never been in a chapel before and I wasn't sure what it was for. While we were on the upper floor, examining the dormitories, the corridors erupted with the clamour of voices: children were swarming into the house below. Those who came across my sister and me stopped and gawped at us as if we were a pair of baboons, the way children aren't at all embarrassed to do. By the time we returned to the big dining room, there they all were, children of every shape, size and hair colouring, dozens and dozens of them, sitting down at the tables, silent at the sight of two alien creatures. Every pair of eyes in the room was on us.

My sister was steered towards a table for girls and boys her own size while I was seated at one with those who were mine.

The older girl in charge of the little ones laid a place for me. I looked around for my sister, because I wanted to stay with her, but she had gone – and she never really came back.

'*Boy! Sit round!*'

Before we were allowed to eat we had to put our hands together and say thank you to Our Lord Jesus for what we were about to receive. This was something I had never done before so I just sat and watched. The girl on the chair next to mine leant towards me and whispered in my ear: 'Don't you believe in God, boy?'

'No.'

'Do you like Satan?'

This word, which was new to me, sounded as if it might be something we were about to receive, like porridge or kedgeree. Because I was hungry and didn't want to miss anything that was going, I nodded.

'Not half!'

The girl looked at me, eyes wide. She nudged her neighbour.

'The new boy don't believe in God,' she told her. 'He likes *Satan*!'

This news travelled round the table. Each child, on receipt of it, gazed at me in horror.

After tea we were shepherded into the chapel where we talked to Our Lord Jesus again, then we were led upstairs to the dormitories where we were to sleep. At the top of the stairs my sister was taken one way and I the other, she towards the back of the house to the room for middle-sized girls, me to the room for the little ones, which was at the front. This room was large with a high ceiling and tall casement windows that had cream-painted shutters folded back. Early evening light filled the whole room. At the height of the picture-rail rabbits and squirrels romped along a frieze. There was a framed picture on the wall of a man with a beard sitting on a donkey. Through the window, beyond the garden, on the far side of the golf course that stretched to the cliff edge, the sky-blue sea edged into a sea-blue sky that was beginning to turn violet. The bed allocated to me, almost as high as my shoulder, was one of a dozen identical iron-framed beds a yard apart, each at right angles to the wall. Next to each bed was an identical wooden cupboard. The floor was polished parquet. The first thing I had noticed about the house was the smell of wax and how polished and clean it was. Accustomed to the comfy clutter of Gloucester Terrace, I was unnerved by the austere tidiness of this place.

Brodie pulled to the wooden shutters and the room became dark. By the light entering the room from the corridor landing she undressed me and put me into a pair of ironed striped pyjamas. She showed me how to kneel down, hold my hands together and say thank you to Our Lord Jesus for everything He had done for me. She tried to take my car out of my hands but I wasn't having it. She wheedled and cajoled but I wouldn't let her have it. In the end, when she saw I was prepared to cry, she gave up and let me get into bed with it. Once I had been slotted between the stiff sheets like a letter into an envelope, I told Brodie I wanted to sleep with my sister, as I did at home. This was out of the question, Brodie said. Boys must never sleep with girls.

'Why not?'

'It's not right.'

'Why isn't it?'

'It's a Sin.'

'What's a Sin?'

'Don't you know?'

'No.'

'A Sin is a moral offence in the eyes of God.'

I told her I wanted my mummy.

'Nobody here has a mummy, my dear.'

'*I* have.'

'Have you?'

'Yes.'

'Are you sure?'

I nodded, fairly sure.

'If you had a mummy, you wouldn't be here.'

For all that we were living under the same roof, my sister and I seldom found ourselves in each other's company. At Church Army Homes for Motherless Children boys and girls were kept apart horizontally by gender and vertically by age and size, like buttons in a tray. She contrived to be near me and talk to me when the opportunity presented itself, which was whenever our paths happened to cross. Different boundaries and routines separated us. Cross-gender intercourse wasn't encouraged, even between siblings. There were older girls among us but no older boys. It was a policy of the Church Army that brothers were sent to a separate establishment for boys only, away from their sisters, as soon as they reached their thirteenth birthday, so I had some way to go yet.

I missed my sister but I also missed my car, which had finally been prised out of my grasp. The injustice of this was obvious to me but when I looked around for a higher authority to appeal to I found myself peering into the ash-coloured eyes of Sister Holmwood, who was holding my car in her hands.

'No one needs his own special toy,' she said. 'All the toys here belong to all the children. You can play with your car whenever you wish.'

But I couldn't carry it around. I couldn't take it to bed with me. I couldn't stop anyone else from playing with it. Brodie, the youngest of the women and the one with the warmest heart, had given me a bear to sleep with, which she said I should keep in my bed. I mustn't take it out of the dormitory. I didn't want Brodie's bear. I wanted my car. I wanted my golly. After a night without either I gave in and went to sleep with the bear, which in the end I grew fond of and I gave the name Bedser.

In due course I reconnoitred the grounds. I explored the long grass at the end of the garden and took a close look at the flint wall that had pieces of green bottle glass cemented into the top of it. The earth banked up in one corner of the garden and there, if I stood on tiptoe, I could see where the blue of the sea met the blue of the sky, the white sails of yachts and the tops of vans that passed on the side of the wall where people went about their business without giving any indication that they knew of our existence. The iron gate with sharp arrow-shaped spikes along it was rarely opened. On those occasions we left the grounds – when we went to school or to church – we used the wooden gate in the wall in the back garden.

Each morning after breakfast and each afternoon after tea we filed into the chapel and knelt on the floorboards to thank Our Lord Jesus for looking after us, although I didn't think He had done a particularly good job in my case. The best thing about Prayers was that while you prayed the gaps between the polished floorboards made interesting ridges in the skin of your knees. My friend Gregory and I knelt side-by-side, pressing down our knees into the gaps. We compared the ridges in our knees while Sister Holmwood told us how much Jesus loved little children; that it was our fault He had died and that His father was God and Mary was our mother. I couldn't see how she could be. For one thing, Mary wasn't as pretty as our mum. Every day we said the words *Our Father, which art in Heaven. Harold be thy name* . . . But that wasn't our father's name, which was Luke, although his friends called him Fergie – and he wasn't in that Heaven place they said he was. He was almost certainly in Bayswater, either at his drawing board or propping up the bar of the Victoria and Albert.

I knew who the Father was – and the Son. But what on earth was the Holy Goat?

After prayers in the chapel on Sunday – which, here, was called the Sabbath – we were dressed in our best clothes and walked to church. In the afternoon we returned to the church hall for Sunday School, where a pretty lady called Miss Grace told us stories about Jesus and his Disciples; how Jesus had showed Simon-called-Peter how to walk on water; and then she asked us questions. You had to give the right answer if you wanted one of the coloured adhesive pictures she handed out for your scrapbook. Once, after I had failed to answer her question right, I burst into tears and Miss Grace took me on her lap and let me cry, my head resting against her bosoms.

At bedtime those children who had not been bad during the week were allowed to choose a chocolate from Sister Slater's box. If you were one of those who had been bad you watched the good children unwrapping and eating their chocolate; if you had been good, you watched the bad children watching you eat it. After brushing our teeth we knelt next to our beds, put our hands together and thanked Jesus for looking after us.

In church, gazing down at the lozenges of brilliant coloured light on the flagstones was almost as much fun as watching the test card on Violet's television set – or, up at the mysterious scenes in the stained-glass windows themselves which was a bit like watching a programme. But when you watched television you had the opportunity to stretch out, yawn, lie down, fart, if you felt like it. You could get up and go to the toilet or eat Vi's shop-bought cakes or just shut your eyes and take a nap. In church you weren't allowed to do any of these things. You mustn't turn round, cough, talk to the person next to you, pick your nose. You had to hold your tongue, keep your head still for several hours without looking in any direction except towards the man in the white frock. If your attention strayed anywhere else, a knuckle rapped against the side of your head like a conker against another conker.

In the wooden pews children were ranked according to height. We stood up and sang hymns, then we sat down and listened while the man in the frock read to us from his book and then we all said *Our Men*. Then, kneeling on little embroidered cushions, we prayed. Praying was something everybody, the sisters and the other children, knew how to do. Because nobody had ever shown me how to pray, I pretended to pray and hoped that nobody would notice. It seemed to me that it was difficult to tell the difference between a person who was praying and a person who was thinking about what was for lunch.

Church was a lonely place. Even though there were hundreds of people with you, families of grown-ups and children, you were always alone because you could never talk to anyone or even look at them. You were left with your own thoughts. Instead of talking to Jesus, I watched the pictures in my mind's eye. I helped my mum make a fruit pie at the kitchen table in the flat in Gloucester Terrace, laughed with her in the dark in the Roxy cinema in Westbourne Grove, played draughts with Dad in the garage, listened to the cricket commentary on the wireless with my brother. I didn't want to let go of these memories any more than I wanted to let go of my car. I surveyed empty fountains in the dead of winter.

Bit into brown sugar sandwiches. Looked down, safe in my dad's arms, onto roiling green water crashing against the piles of the bridge over the Serpentine. Watched the pretty pattern the paraffin stove made on the ceiling at night.

Instead of praying, I thought about Mum and Dad and my brother, and all the things that had happened in my life. I had noticed recently how rapidly the present mutated into the past. If I wanted to keep hold of my past, I would have to think about it all the time, as Dad did. The period designated for prayer was a convenient time to do this.

My car had been placed in the box of cars that was kept in one of the cupboards in the nursery, where all the toys were. There was a box for building bricks, a box for the castle and soldiers, a box for dolls and the dolls' house. A dressing-up box. At different times some of the boxes were taken out so that we could play with the toys which, afterwards, were put back into the boxes and returned to the cupboards. The toys were distributed randomly at set times in the day, which meant that you couldn't go to them when you felt like it, when you needed them.

Whenever the opportunity presented itself I made a beeline for my MG roadster, although I wasn't allowed to play with it all the time, to have exclusive use of it. That wouldn't have been fair because, according to Our Lord Jesus, we must share our things with each other. I had to let other boys play with my MG sometimes and, besides, there were plenty of other cars in the box. My strategy was to get hold of one of these cars, sidle up to the boy playing with my MG, which had lost its tyres and some of its paintwork, and make a switch, either through negotiation or by prising it out of his grasp finger by finger until he let go of it. This wasn't always easy under the beady-eyed supervision of the sister on duty.

One wet afternoon I came upon my friend Gregory driving my car a little bit too recklessly, I thought, mashing the front mudguard against the wooden skirting-board. I tried to persuade Gregory to race the car I was holding but he wasn't interested. When it was clear he wasn't going to take the bait, I kicked him in the ribs a couple of times as hard as I could. That did the trick. Gregory soon let go of the MG.

Seized, I was frog-marched into the presence of the head Sister, who received an account of what had taken place in the playroom. Sister Slater, without saying a word to me, led me by the hand into the chapel and shut the door behind me so that we were alone with each other and the picture of Our Lord Jesus welcoming the little children unto him. She sat down on one of the straw-bottomed chairs that were like the ones Mr Szymynski mended at the end of the mews in Bayswater. She put me over her knee, pulled down my shorts and pants and slapped my bare arse with one of my own plimsolls until I howled.

'There, boy!' Sister Slater said. She handed me back my plimsoll. 'Perhaps that will teach you not to be so violent!'

My sister came running like a feral creature as soon as she heard me howling, although she was prevented from comforting me. She was sent back to the room for middle-sized girls, tearful herself.

My sister found the experience of being a subject of this regime more distressing than I did. She was more disorientated, having lost the thread of her life's quest to discover her reason for being. Individual identity was frowned upon under the Church Army's strict regimen, as it is in a real army. She was desolate. Being older, she was expected to toe the line more assiduously than an infant. For her, the Path of Righteousness was narrower and, when she strayed from it, the Act of Atonement proportionately more arduous. She accepted her fate with leaden despair. She learnt to hold her pen in her right hand, since there were no left-handed children at the Home, as there was no child whose hair wasn't parted on the left. In spite of being younger – or for that reason – I tended to take a less desperate view of our situation than she did. Dad had said he would come back and fetch us. It never crossed my mind that he wouldn't do this.

After the incident with Gregory I got the impression that I was being watched. I was given less opportunity to play with my car, whereas other boys were free to take hold of it and see how far the passenger door opened as much they pleased, and if I made a fuss I was spoken to. By a stroke of luck one afternoon I came across my dear old MG upside-down on the nursery floor where some boy had abandoned it. One of the doors was off. The suspension was gone. It was a shame how much swank it had lost. I managed to smuggle the car out of the house and into the garden. Although taking toys outside was forbidden, it was easy enough to do. In the little ditch where the earth was loose before it banked between the hedge and the flint wall rimmed with bottle glass, I scraped a shallow grave and buried my car, covering it with earth, stones and leaves. I promised myself I would return one day and repossess it.

After I had carried out this pagan act, I felt a weight had been lifted from me. The battle was over. Having shed the thing I loved most, I was less vulnerable, better able to face the Invisible Forces of Darkness. My car was beyond Their reach and therefore so was I.

At the Home there was an unwritten list of rules to be learnt and remembered. Every morning we were to fold our pyjamas neatly on top of our bedside cupboard and stand by our beds for them to be inspected. Each item of our clothing was numbered and we were only to wear garments with our own number on them. My number was 56. One or two of the older sisters sometimes absent-mindedly referred to us by our numbers: *Fifty-six! Do not eat your snot!* Things that had been allowed in Gloucester Terrace were forbidden: lying on your bed in the afternoon picking your feet; sauntering into the kitchen, hands in pockets, to see what was cooking; sitting on the toilet for half an hour looking at a comic. You were supposed to be quiet in the house and never run. You couldn't curl up on the sofa next to the radio to listen to *Paul Temple* because there was no radio and no sofa. You might be engaged in some perfectly normal pursuit, racing a gob of your spit down a window pane against your friend Gregory's, for example, when, without warning, a pair of fingers clamped your earlobe and rotated your head through ninety degrees so that you came face to face with an old lady with grey eyes. If you ate your snot or played with your food or said bad things to another child, you were stood on the table in the room and slapped on the back of the leg to teach you a lesson; you were left to stand there until you had stopped snivelling. If you were bad at night, especially if you were found touching your tossel, you were told to take a blanket into the corridor and sleep all night on the polished parquet floor outside Sister Slater's room.

Beyond the bounded territory of the Home, on the far side of the glass-topped wall, was the perilous natural world, the traffic of strangers, the sea, an unpredictable clutter that must never be allowed to cross the boundary and disrupt the grid of rituals that secured us within our special status, as dirt must not enter the body. If you weren't vigilant, if you crossed your knife and fork instead of laying them side by side on the table, if you failed to finish a prayer once you had started it, if you touched your tossel at night, if you peed in your bed, Satan would seize his chance. He would trick you and you would go to Hell. Satan was a trickster, an old charmer with a wicked smile who promised more than he could deliver, who sowed discord and heartbreak and who hated God. He sounded reassuringly familiar to me.

The sisters who looked after us, patrolling the frontier between Good and Evil on our behalf, hardly ever smiled or saw the funny side of things and, except for Brodie, they never laughed. They had enlisted in the army of Our Lord Jesus in order to pass on his teaching to the unwanted children of feckless women who, like Mary, had not been married to the father of their offspring. The sisters didn't go home after work because they had no other home, no family or husbands or children of their own to go to. Each slept in her own room, which had a single bed in it and on the wall a wooden cross with an ivory model of Jesus nailed to it. This house was their home as much as it was ours. Here, like us, they were safe from the world on the far side of the perimeter wall.

Some children, those who had arrived as babies, had lived here all their life. It was all they had ever known and so they were better informed than I was on the subjects of Jesus and Mary, Satan, Sin, Punishment, Atonement and Redemption, that were woven into the workings of the Home. Letting your pee stain your underpants yellow, for example, was a Sin – a moral offence in the eyes of God – for which missing the visit to the annual Babbacombe Fair was the appropriate Act of Atonement. Because I had let my pee stain my underpants yellow, I lay in the dark – alone in the dormitory with Bedser my bear and the Holy Goat, listening to the distant amplified merry-go-round music coming from the cliff-side of

Babbacombe – until my coevals returned from the fair, noisy and excited, sh-sh-ed by Brodie in order not to wake me.

My life was made easier by Sylvia, the girl who had been shocked to hear that I liked Satan. Sylvia, because she had been an inmate at the Home all her life, understood how the place worked and she took it upon herself to induct me into its secret ways. Sylvia hardly ever Transgressed, because she knew what Sin was. She knew all about Satan. In the greenhouse where old Mr Woodfall kept his seedlings in winter and his bedding plants in spring, she put my hand up her dress and under her knickers into the place between her legs where, just as with mum and my sister, something was missing, while her own cool hand clasped my hot tossel.

Sylvia looked after me. We lolled against each other in the outside toilet while rain drummed on the wooden roof. At bath time, alone together in the bathroom, she danced for me without a towel. She knew what I wanted to see before I knew myself. She held my hand in the crocodile of infants that wended its way every weekday to school.

Babbacombe Primary was an ordinary local authority school and the teachers made no distinction between Sylvia and Gregory and me and the local boys and girls. Here we weren't different to anybody else. Now that I didn't have a patch over one eye and I could see the blackboard and follow the lesson, I was able to read the books and do the sums. Our teacher, Mr O'Sweetie, was very tall and smoked a pipe. He had an identical twin brother, also called Mr O'Sweetie, who was also very tall and also smoked a pipe and who sometimes came into school to teach us when his brother had to go fishing with his friend, Captain Cod. We loved both Mr O'Sweeties. They made us laugh, although never at the same time.

During the week before Bonfire Night Mr Woodfall built a bonfire on the front lawn and, to our cheers, the effigy of Guy Fawkes, who was a Catholic, made by the big girls, was placed on top of it. After tea on the Fifth of November we were each given a toffee apple and, while we sank our remaining milk teeth into these, we watched the bonfire being lit through the French windows. As soon as we had finished our toffee apples we could go outside and watch the fireworks – but not before. We must finish our toffee apple – quickly, hating it – before we could put on our coat and gloves and step out and smell the gunpowder.

I frequently missed my mum while I was at the Home but it was on occasions such as this that I missed my dad, who would have told the sisters what they could do with their bloody toffee apple.

Towards Christmas, the infants at the school began to prepare for the Nativity play. I was assigned the part of one of several shepherds who came to Bethlehem to see for themselves the baby Jesus lying in a manger. I wore the costume of a Galilee shepherd, a long tunic and a headdress, and I carried a wooden staff. After the final rehearsal, in the afternoon of the play's performance, we returned home for tea still wearing our costumes – and, in my case, a charcoal moustache and beard – because we would only have to change back into them for the performance later. After I had finished my tea, while I was in the garden, I saw the opportunity I had been waiting for. I looked around to see whether I was being observed. It didn't look as if I was. The garden was deserted. If I escaped from the Home now, I would be able to make my way back to Gloucester Terrace because nobody would ever recognise me in my shepherd's costume, my Galilee headdress, moustache and beard. In such a disguise I would easily evade capture. I didn't want to be *inside* any more and the temptation to be *outside* overwhelmed me. I wanted to be at large, as I had once been at large in Kensington Gardens. I wasn't afraid of Satan. The fact was, I was rather missing him.

Daunted by the shards of glass on the perimeter wall, I climbed the iron gate. It was easy to get both feet onto the crossbar. From there I had to put one leg over the top, place it between the spikes, and then, transferring my weight to that leg, swing the other over. I managed to do this all right. It was when it became necessary to lift my leg onto the far side that I got into difficulties. The spikes became entangled in my shepherd's costume, my foot slipped and the underside of my thigh slid onto the sharp point of one of the spikes, which speared into the flesh several inches.

For a moment I was stuck fast, my leg impaled on the iron gate. I couldn't move. I daren't cry out, reluctant to call to my assistance those I wished to escape from. I gave myself permission to sob quietly to myself until a pair of strong hands – they belonged to my friend, Mr Woodfall – carefully lifted me off the spike and carried me into the house. I was laid on my tummy in the sickroom and, while I waited for Retribution to strike, my wound was examined. Not only had I Transgressed, I had been caught in the Act of Transgression. I had tried to breach the border between the closed world of Our Lord Jesus, who wasn't our father, and the abominated realm of Satan, who was.

But the seriousness of my wound was a matter of some concern to Sister Slater and Sister Holmwood. They didn't like the look of it and a doctor was sent for. He arrived and cracked jokes while he sewed me up, impressed by my sang froid as he did this. He didn't understand that what allowed me to make light of his needle was the fear of what was going follow later, after he had left.

'You'll have a scar there, my boy,' he said, as if it was something I should be glad to have.

And he was right, I did. I carried a scar on the back of my thigh for the rest of my life, and I *was* glad to have it because it proved that my memory of this event was true. My scar would always be there to remind me that this had happened.

Sewn up, I was put to bed on my tummy, with the result that I was unable to take part in the Nativity play, just then getting under way. I hadn't escaped the Home and I had missed the opportunity of being present at the birth of Baby Jesus, something I had been rather looking forward to.

In spring we walked to the woods above Babbacombe and picked bluebells and primroses. On Palm Sunday we were each given a cross made out of palm leaves in remembrance of Jesus's entry into Jerusalem on a donkey. I was taken by Brodie on a bus to an optician in Brixham, who tested my eyes and made me a new pair of glasses. At last, one gorgeously hot day in July we walked in a straggling crocodile down the steep zig-zaggy road cut into the cliff next to the golf course to Babbacombe beach. It was a wonderful moment when we emerged out of the cool broken shade of the wooded road into the blinding light of the beach. The red cliffs. The blue sea. The white sand already crowded with holidaymakers. Our troupe arrived in double file, chanting in unison:

Onward, Christian Soldiers,
Marching as to war,
With the cross of Jesus
Going on before.

The silver and maroon flag of the Church Army was carried aloft and then planted in the sand, staking out our claim to a separate identity.

We – me, Sylvia, Gregory, all the little ones – changed into our swimming costumes as fast as we could and ran into the water and splashed each other, almost drowning in the excitement. My sister and I got to use our tin buckets and spades, just as Dad had given us to suppose we would. I was happy to watch the big girls in their big girls' bathing costumes, their hair in swimming caps, tossing our plastic beach ball to and fro, leaping up for it, squealing with laughter. Then we took donkey-rides along the beach. Brodie traced with her finger the cross on the donkey's back and explained that he had got this from carrying Jesus of Nazareth into Jerusalem. He was an old donkey.

Another Bonfire Night, another birthday, another Christmas, another Nativity play. But not another spring. In February, Dad arrived out of the blue. He had telephoned to say he was on his way to pick us up and we were fetched from school and got ready. The car nosing through the gates wasn't Old Mother Riley, but a lovely dove-grey 3-litre Alvis saloon.

'Hello, you two!' he said, grinning down at us as if it had been only a couple of weeks ago that he had left us here. 'I've come to take you home!'

My sister and I – we were in no particular hurry to approach him – looked up into the blue-grey eyes of an old man with white hair, bald pate and unnaturally white-toothed smile, who claimed to be our father.

Dad was in a tearing hurry to set off immediately, so we were denied the opportunity of saying goodbye to anyone – to Brodie, of whom we had grown fond, to my friends Gregory and Sylvia, to Mr O'Sweetie or Mr O'Sweetie's brother, to Mr Woodfall, or even to my bear Bedser, which stayed behind on my pillow – or to anyone my sister had formed a relationship with. He wanted to get back on the road again as soon as possible. Our departure was as abrupt as our arrival had been eighteen months before. One moment we were in the vestibule of the Home, the next we were in a beautiful motor car, the big engine firing. It was him all right. As we drove away from the grounds, past the mud-coloured sea on one side, the glass-topped flint wall on the other, I remembered that I was leaving behind, rusting to bits in the earth but in my mind's eye as full of swank as ever, my MG roadster.

Dad drove us back to London. By the time we reached our destination it was already dark and he carried me, sleepy, into our new home, a converted horse stables in Addison Road, where our mum, laughing through her tears, was waiting for us with open arms and bowls of hot soup with squares of fried bread in it. For pudding an apple crumble with fresh cream.

After she had tucked us up in our own beds in our own bedrooms, she kissed us goodnight.

Three Quests

Our new home lay behind an ugly brown 1930s block of flats that was wedged between elegant white-stuccoed Victorian mansions like a discoloured tooth in an otherwise perfect set. To reach it, you stepped down into a passage that led under the block of flats and came out into a narrow courtyard Mum called *the area*, where the dustbins and coal for the flats were stored. Enclosing the area, facing you, was the L of an old stables that had been built to service the Victorian mansions. Our living quarters were the top half of the L. Underneath these were the abandoned cobbled stables with stalls for the horses, which still contained some of their feeding boxes, harnesses, odd bits of tackle, and their smell. Generations of nags had pissed here. My room must have been where feed was stored because under the floorboards – where I kept my spud gun – were ancient dusty oats and the window was the top half of a Dutch door, the lower half of which had been nailed shut. In the area a rope hand-pulley affixed to the rear of the block of flats lowered down the rubbish and hoisted the empty bins and, in winter, the scuttles full of coal or ashes. Every morning at eight o'clock, whatever the weather, Dad did this and once a week Mum hoovered the carpets of the stairs and polished the brasses on the doors to the flats. For carrying out these chores they were allowed to live rent-free in the rotting but rather picturesque flat over the old stables. The building may have been rotting but the address in Holland Park was a good one. Dad was chuffed to be able to put a PARk telephone number on his business card, which was not as good as MAYfair but better than BAYswater or NOTting Hill or PADdington.

W.L.G. Ferguson
Mechanical Design Engineer
96 Addison Road
London W14
PARk 2674

The card was handy because it could be taken out of a pigskin leather wallet and placed like a trump along with the cheque on top of a bill for goods received or services rendered.

My brother returned home for the school holidays and then we were a family again. I had almost forgotten what he looked like. He wasn't as tall as Dad yet, but he would be soon, so he wasn't so easy to push around, and he possessed an even more heroic profile than I remembered. We had to get to know each other all over again. He was easy-going with me but I held no surprises for him. His LCC boarding school in an eighteenth-century mansion overlooking the River Orwell in Suffolk was a place of adventure and enchantment, whereas the dismal house on the cliffs of Babbacombe in Devon where my sister and I had been parked was hardly worth talking about. The circumstances of my life were not as interesting as his – and they never would be.

The year and a half my sister and I had spent in a Church Army Home, with its bizarre rituals and punishments, what we had done and what had been done to us, was of no interest to any of the other members of our family. They asked no questions about it and they never found out what it had been like for us. Eventually, we stopped making any reference to it. Our time there became like the pages of a book that had stuck together so that the words written on them were impossible to read. That section of the story was lost.

Mum – her TB cured by the brand-new wonder drug streptomycin – had a job in the Lyons' factory, Cadby Hall, in Olympia, from where she sometimes brought home boxes of Lyon's mini chocolate-covered Swiss rolls wrapped in silver paper. By now she understood that if she was to live with Fergie she would need her own income – or she wouldn't get any money at all. Whether or not she minded working, she was grateful to be alive and to have her family with her again. On Sunday afternoons, in front of the fire with slices of cinnamon toast, she read to me and my sister *The Adventures of Huckleberry Finn*, giving Jim and the Niggers the voices of Scousers. She wasn't ill any more but she wasn't strong either. Because she had only one kidney, she needed to get up several times in the night to pee.

We all rubbed along with each other, although our tastes and interests were completely different. Dad had acquired a three-speed record-player on which he played his Jean Sablon 78s – 'Vous qui passez sans me voir' – and his collection of dance band records; Mum Frank Sinatra's LP *In the Wee Small Hours*; my sister – the end of her quest almost in sight – Elvis Presley and Ricky Nelson; my brother Bix Beiderbecke, Big Bill Broonzy and his LP of Dylan Thomas reading his own poems – *Grief, thief of time . . . And Death shall have no dominion . . . Do not go gentle into that good night . . .* – whose baffling splendour haunted me, then and for ever.

While I was getting to know our new home I let myself into the block of flats Dad was responsible for and took a butcher's. It was posh. On a carpeted landing half-way up the carpeted stairs, at the back of the building, a sash window opened onto the slate roof of our flat over the stables. I climbed out of the window and, seeing no reason to turn back, made my way along the guttering of the roof, which was just wide enough for a boy to walk along if he was careful to place one plimsolled foot in front of the other. The lead gutter affixed to the wall beneath the tiles was sturdy enough to take my weight. On one side was the upward pitch of the roof; on the other, a sheer drop into somebody's garden thirty or forty feet below, so it wasn't a good idea to lean too far over in that direction. After having walked almost the length of the guttering I arrived at a skylight set into the slate roof and I looked down through the unwashed glass into the room below. It was somebody's bedroom. The light was on and a beautiful woman was sitting at her dressing table in her brassiere and petticoat, a cigarette burning in the ashtray. She was applying lipstick to her lips, forming them into pretty cupid shapes in her mirror as if rehearsing how to make kisses. She did this several times, then she lifted the cigarette to her mouth, inhaled and replaced it in the ashtray. I watched her for several moments, absorbed in the novel experience of observing a beautiful woman without being seen by her. It was exciting to be on the outside, looking in; to know and not be known. Eventually, I tapped on the skylight window to attract the woman's attention.

Mum, startled, looked up at me over her shoulder. I grinned and waved, but *she* didn't. She wasn't as pleased to see me as I thought she should be. Her mouth opened, although through the paint-sealed skylight I couldn't quite hear what she was saying. Her arms were flapping. It was like looking down onto a person trapped underwater, drowning. She grabbed her dressing-gown and ran out of the room. By the time I had turned through ninety degrees and inched my way back along the guttering, she was standing at the open window, waiting for me. She grabbed me by the scruff of the neck, pulled me roughly through the window and held me so hard it hurt. Her tears, her anger, her painful hugs: it was like the business with the knife-grinder all over again. I couldn't see why she was carrying on like this. It wasn't as if I was dead or anything, was it?

My new school was in Hammersmith, Lena Gardens Primary, between Shepherd's Bush Road and the above-ground section of the Metropolitan Line. Except for a coloured boy from the Gold Coast – like me, a stranger amid the alien corn – the children were white working-class cockneys, with some Irish thrown in, mostly from the surrounding terraced streets, whose parents all knew each other and who drank in the same pubs, having attended the school themselves before the War. My classmates all had nans, watched television every night, supported QPR or Fulham, fished in the reservoir on Sundays with their dads, and collected bus numbers. I had nothing in common with any of them. We had no television at home and I had never seen *Wagon Train* or *Double Your Money*. I had no nan. I had never been to Loftus Road or Craven Cottage. The boys were as hard as nails and gave no quarter. Their elder brothers were called Teddy boys who, the *Daily Mirror* alleged, carried razors and had fights outside the Hammersmith Palais on Saturday nights. I had to fight every one of my classmates before I was admitted into the tribe. When I fought I was an awkward customer because I didn't know how to submit. Having done a stretch in a Christian children's home, I was capable of inflicting and withstanding a degree of pain far beyond anything they could imagine. I sometimes fought my adversary in a greeny-red Grant tartan kilt, which I wore to school because, in Dad's opinion, I wasn't a working-class Londoner; I was the son of a Scot. In Shepherd's Bush and Hammersmith there were some Irish who were called Micks, one or two Jews we called Yids, a few West Indians called Spades, and some Poles, who were just Poles. If there were any other Scots wearing kilts, I never saw them.

In my second-to-last year at Lena Gardens there were two classes, a top class for those who would go to grammar school when they passed the 11-plus, and a lower class for those earmarked for the secondary modern. I was in the lower class. Our teacher was Mr Jones, who kept a bamboo cane he called Brother Sunshine on the ledge over the blackboard. Boys who overstepped the mark were invited to come up to the front of the class, smirking to their mates, to bend over and touch their toes to receive a couple of swipes from Brother Sunshine. Girls were never caned; they were sent to the headmaster, who wrote their name in the Cane Book, which was usually enough to make them cry. It was preferable to renew your acquaintance with Brother Sunshine in a pleated kilt, I found, than in thin grey flannel trousers.

At the end of term, a photographer came into school and we each had our photograph taken for Christmas. In mine I'm still wearing my Remembrance Day poppy – *Lest We Forget* – and a Ferguson tartan tie because our name now was Ferguson.

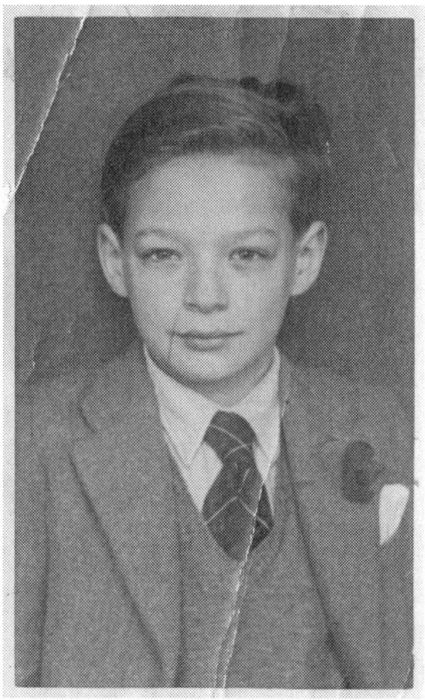

I am not wearing my glasses in my photo because I never wore my glasses at this school. If this meant I couldn't see what Mr Jones had written on the blackboard, at least I wasn't a four-eyes. I could square up to an adversary when the situation required me to. I could see the whites of his eyes.

On Friday mornings, when we had Scottish country dancing in the hall, I usually found a way to stand close to Jean Watts when partners were chosen so that I could get my hands on her. Scottish country dancing gave me a pretext to clasp her fingers in mine, place my hand against her frock on the slope of her waist and hold her tight as we reeled the length of the hall. Twirling in such close proximity to Jean Watts, the blood pumping through my veins, I seemed to understand what girls were *for*. Although this one possessed the usual mysterious attributes of the chosen girl – the pretty hair, the soft mouth, the smooth skin smelling of soap, the fluffy candyfloss-pink angora cardigan – it was, at this school, unknown for boys to have girls for friends. Girls played in separate sections of the playground from the boys. They were different. To be told to sit next to one in class was a punishment. Girls – who, it was generally supposed, had two bottoms, one at the back and one at the front – tucked the hem of their dresses into their knickers and did handstands against the wall, bounced balls under their leg and skipped over ropes, chanting nonsense. They walked arm-in-arm in groups of three or four. They plaited each other's hair. Those of us who had only one bottom and a willie played ball games: football, cricket and kingy, in which a tennis ball was thrown as hard as possible at the legs of a running target. Girls talked. Boys fought.

Playground fights erupted over any trivial disagreement – while the chant went up: *Fight! Fight! Fight!* – and these were broken up by the member of staff who was drinking her cup of tea on playground duty. The more serious fights were those between boys who decided to dispute each other's position in the hierarchy of toughness. A muttered challenge was made from one of the two – *See you after school for a fight* – or from one of their mates, who acted as seconds. If the challenge was accepted, the adversaries met just outside the gates when school finished and cold-bloodedly entered into combat. Such fights were all about honour. There was no kicking or biting, hardly any punching; opposing supporters cheered and urged on their champion but they didn't interfere and they made sure there was no foul play. A fight was a scraggy wrestle and usually the victorious boy was the one who succeeded in kneeling on his opponent's shoulders or, gaining a headlock on him, squeezing his neck until he couldn't breathe. The fight was over as soon as one of the combatants said it was or when one of the women came out of her house and pulled the two boys apart. On receipt of a challenge the dread of the encounter hung over you throughout the balance of the school day until the moment of truth arrived. Refusal meant a humiliating relegation into that mass of weedy, fat or four-eyed boys who didn't fight, who were called *girls*.

After a preliminary ritual push and shove and stand off, I made an agreement with a tough called Brian Smith, *Smiffy*, to fight after school. I met Smiffy outside the school gates, he with his cohort of pals, me with the coloured boy from the Gold Coast who had agreed to hold my jacket. I fought Smiffy because he had found out – obviously from one of the girls who had told him – that I was soft on Jean Watts. To be soft on a girl was almost as degrading to a boy's reputation as to refuse a challenge to fight. I had no choice. Smiffy had held up to public scrutiny my private obsession about this girl. I was being jeered. The only way I could put a stop to this slur on my reputation was to fight him.

Smiffy and I wrestled each other to the ground. Using his extra weight he soon got on top of me and held me down with his knees on my forearms. This was considered an impossible grip to get out of but, with my legs straight, I bent double and hooked my ankles round Smiffy's neck, then pulled his head back so that he was obliged to change his position if he didn't want his spine to snap. It was an advantage, I always found, to fight in a kilt a boy in long trousers. In addition to the tartan's natural warlike properties, it gave greater room for manoeuvre. I soon got Smiffy's head under my arm and I squeezed his neck until his eyes were popping out of his head. Luckily for him one of the women came out of her house and broke our fight up before I had a chance to choke the living daylights out of him.

But Smiffy was right; I *was* soft on Jean Watts. I thought about her all the time. The image of this girl filled a gap in my life. I needed her – but what did I need her for? As far as I could tell, other boys didn't succumb to this sort of obsessive interest in a girl. It wasn't something you could talk about to your mates or to members of your family. I was puzzled by the intensity of this bewildering, pointless desire. It was a faintly guilty secret.

During one half-term holiday, Jean Watts's family moved from Sulgrave Road in Shepherd's Bush to a place called Perivale, because her father had got a job there. Overnight Jean disappeared out of my life. I had held her in my arms during Scottish country dancing for the last time.

Perivale, I found out from the Underground map, was beyond Ealing, almost at the end of the Central Line. One Saturday morning I put my bike on the train at Shepherd's Bush Green and took it to Perivale, where I cycled around the almost deserted rows of identical suburban houses, the red-brick gabled High Street, the charmless little park, in the hope of catching sight of Jean Watts in her fluffy candyfloss-pink angora sweater.

And if I had seen her and if she had seen me, what did I think was going to happen? What was I going to say to her? *Hello, Jean Watts? Fancy meeting you! I just happened to be cycling round Perivale High Street, five miles from where I live.* I didn't know why I was looking for her. I didn't understand what I wanted her to do.

After an hour or so of this I gave up, took the train home and began to get used to life without Jean Watts.

One October evening Dad took me into the flats, up the hoovered carpeted stairs, past the doors with polished brass bells and knobs, to the top floor and a little hatch we reached by means of a metal ladder fixed to the wall. With a key he unlocked the hatch and we climbed through it into the cold air onto the flat tarmacked roof. We were high up, much higher than the tips of the plane trees in the street and the communal gardens below. Cautiously leaning over the edge, because there was no guard rail, we looked down onto the area and the stables below and, tiny like a dolls' house, the pitched roof of our own home, the gutter I had walked along and the skylight window. But we had not come up to look down but to turn our gaze away from the earth.

Dad said that what we were doing – looking down and then looking up – was what mathematicians do when they change small numbers into large numbers and then convert those large numbers to small numbers again. Looking up at the heavenly bodies – changing these small numbers back into large numbers – was how human beings understood their proper size in the Scheme of Things.

Overhead in the black sky were the stars and the Milky Way. Dad pointed out to me the constellations visible: Pisces, Cassiopeia, Perseus; the planets Saturn and Venus. He knew the names of them all. He pointed out the dot of light under the W of Cassiopeia and explained that this, Andromeda, was not a star but a whole galaxy so distant that the light we saw now was light that had taken zillions of light years to get to earth, from a time before dinosaurs roamed. The silvery crescent moon, low in the sky, was in fact lit by the sun, for the time being out of sight from this side of the earth, reflected back from the moon's surface; the curve of the crescent was the shadow of the earth. There was no mystery about it, if you understood what you were looking at. Although light travelled at 186,000 miles per second, the glimmer from the stars we were looking at had started out at about the time Dad had been a boy my age. By the time the light these stars were emitting tonight reached West London, I would be an old man like him.

After a while, at the exact moment he predicted by his watch, a tiny speck of light from a star could be seen travelling slowly – or rather quickly, if you could do the numbers – across the night sky from the direction of Putney. Strictly speaking, Dad said, it wasn't a star but an artificial moon, a celestial body that hadn't been seen in the night sky over England before this moment since time began.

'That's one in the eye for the Americans,' he said. It seemed to give Dad particular delight that it was the Russians who had got there first. '*And* for the bishops and rabbis!'

Dad was thrilled by this event. The pulsating glimmer crossing the night sky that had been dreamed up by mathematicians and mechanical design engineers was all the confirmation a person needed to know that there was no ghost in the machine.

Half a century before, when the light from these stars had set forth, Dad had stood on Pirn Crag with his brothers Ian and Duncan and observed a Blériot flying machine crossing the sky from one horizon to the other. If the span of his life could encompass both these events, we were going to be on the moon in no time.

We watched the spark of *Sputnik 1* pass overhead, then descend towards North London somewhere in the region of Tottenham Court Road.

'That's something you can tell your grandchildren,' Dad said as we came back down to earth. 'You can say you saw the first space ship!'

A Flâneur

Out of the blue Dad announced to Mum that he had made arrangements for me to visit France for the summer in order for me to learn some French.

'Don't you think he's a bit young?' she objected.

'Phooey! I was younger than he is when *I* went.'

'You were *with your family*! You were *at school*!'

He pooh-poohed her objections. Anyway, there was no point arguing; it was all arranged. A man he knew in the Norland Arms public house had taken a job in Paris and Dad had persuaded him to fix up a place for me to stay. It would do me good to see Paris, he said.

I was smartened up. My hair was cut. Wearing Dad's RN tie, I had my picture taken in a professional photographic studio in Kensington High Street. At Petty France a passport was made for me.

Dad taught me a few phrases of French to be getting along with:

Bonjour monsieur, madame.

Je m'appelle Neil.

Je viens d'Angleterre.

J'ai dix ans.

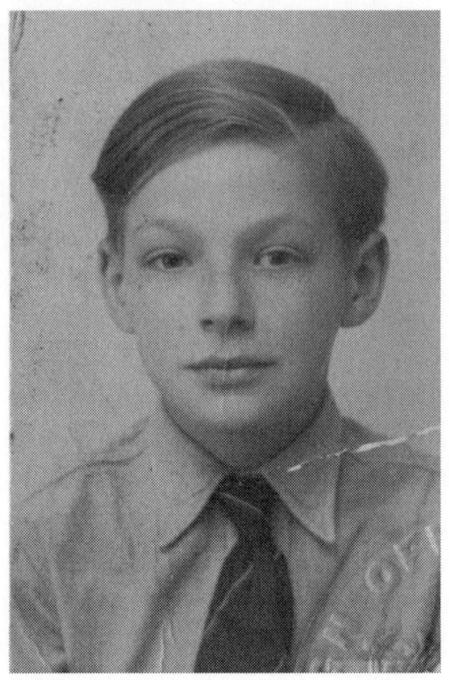

Comment allez-vous?

Au revoir.

I was taken out of school. Carrying a small suitcase containing folded clothes and my brother's box camera, I was driven to London airport where Mum and Dad handed me over to a beautiful air hostess who escorted me onto a plane bound for Paris. One moment the silver BEA four-engined Vickers Viscount was on the runway, looking no bigger than my Matchbox model Hawker Hunter jet fighter; the next, I was walking up steps into it. Then the roar of the Rolls-Royce turbines; then take-off. Then, below, England. Each discrete moment separated me from the moment before. It was an unstoppable process outside my control. In no time at all, *here* had become *there*.

During the flight I watched through the oval window the steel wings of the plane part wisps of cloud as if it were the aircraft that was stationary and the clouds that were drifting past. The American businessman seated next to me was intrigued to learn that I was travelling unaccompanied between England and France. The beautiful air hostess made a fuss of me. She took me into the captain's cabin to meet the pilot, who said, 'Hello, young fellow.'

At Beauvais airport the beautiful BEA hostess handed me over to a man I had never seen before called Jack Grierson, Dad's chum from the Norland Arms public house. He wore a brown suit and a trilby and he was smoking a briar pipe. From the outset I got the impression he was annoyed with me about something. I didn't know what was annoying him and he didn't tell me. Perhaps the task of making arrangements in Paris on my behalf was disagreeable to him.

I spent my first night in Paris near Place Pigalle on a pull-down bed in the cluttered apartment of Madame Célèste, an old lady who gave off a terrible smell and smoked cigarettes she rolled herself in yellow papers. Although she shared her apartment with several cats and she had the appearance of a wicked witch in a fairy story, including hairs sprouting from her face and teeth like the stubbed-out fag ends of her cigarettes, Madame Célèste wasn't a witch. She wasn't wicked at all, but gentle and rather warm-hearted.

In the morning she took me to the local market. She bought me a round two-tier chocolate éclair called *une réligieuse* – which, to her horror, I wolfed down then and there in the street – and a small tortoise, smaller than the palm of my hand, that I put in my pocket. The tortoises, the old lady communicated, were not sold as pets but to be cooked and eaten. Madame Célèste didn't know what to make of me.

It baffled her that I found the dishes she put before me so unappealing. The smells in her apartment, of her cigarettes, of her cats, of herself, and the taste of her food, made me want to gag. All I was prepared to eat were éclairs and *frîtes*. Because neither of us spoke the other's language we were unable to communicate.

An old lady and a *gamin des rues*; it wasn't going to work. After three days Jack Grierson took me away from Place Pigalle in his Citroën, even more annoyed with me than he had been when he had taken me there. He drove me to rue Daunou, a short narrow street that bisected avenue de l'Opéra and rue de la Paix as if truncating the nose of an enormous *tranche* of Brie pointing towards place de l'Opéra. On the way he gave me a good talking-to. My father would be very disappointed, he said, if he were to hear about my uncooperative behaviour. In his talking-to was an implied threat: it was in his power to pass on this information to my dad if my behaviour did not improve. I had no idea what he was talking about.

He led me into a bar, open for business but quiet at this time in the morning. In the rear of the bar *le patron* and his wife shook hands with him and then with me, looking me up and down, nodding and shrugging as if making up their minds whether or not I would do. *Le patron* asked me the only question I knew how to reply to in French:

'*Comment tu t'appelles?*'

'*Je m'appelle Neil.*'

'*Nill?*'

'*Oui.*'

Once it had been decided that I would do, hands were shaken again and Grierson drove off, leaving me in the charge of two people who didn't speak English and whose names I had already forgotten.

Bar Daunou was a long narrow shoe-box shaped space with a *zinc* running along one side and some fixed tables opposite. Every fitting was polished chrome, bright and modern: smart, just the opposite of an English pub. At the front, visible from the street, was a jukebox; at the back, away from the natural light of the big street window, was a pair of American pinball machines. Behind the *zinc* was a young barman in a white jacket; behind the young barman, stacked glasses, rows of bottles of alcohol and brightly coloured *sirops*. This was where I was to stay.

But it wasn't clear to me where I was to sleep. There was a kitchen at the rear of the bar where food was prepared for the clientele, and a toilet for anybody's use. I hung around the bar waiting for something to happen without understanding that nothing more than this was going to happen. This, now, was the situation I was in. While *le patron* and *madame* and the barman went about their business, serving customers, I was left to amuse myself. I drank Coca-Cola for the first time. I played the fabulous American pinball machines – *Bam! B'bam-B'bam! Bam! Tilt! Game over!* – until the young barman thought to show me to my room. We climbed the old staircase at the rear of the building to the sixth floor, beyond the point where the carpet ended and the linoleum began. At the top of the stairs a corridor of rooms under the mansards led in both directions. He opened the door to one of the rooms for me, placed my suitcase on the bed and handed me the Yale key to the door. Then he left for his own room further down the corridor.

The room was simple and clean, with a bed and a table, a small chest of drawers and, in the corner, a washbasin. Instead of a window there was a skylight in the sloping ceiling, too high to look out of but with a rope pulley by which to open and close it. The toilet for the whole corridor was in a cubicle outside my door, the first hole-in-the-floor type of toilet I had seen. I transferred the contents of my suitcase to the chest of drawers and put myself to bed, taking Max with me. Max, I decided, was a name suitable equally for a male or a female tortoise. The darkness of the room framed the rectangle of sky through which the moon shone.

The big difficulty about my new lodgings was knowing what to *do*, to understand what exactly was expected of me. *Le patron* and his wife talked to me as if I knew French. Baffled that I was unable to follow their simple instructions, they shrugged their shoulders at each other as if to say: *The boy's a half-wit.* It took me several days to get the hang of the routines, which tended to centre around meals. For breakfast, a piece of chocolate in bread, *café au lait* in a bowl. After breakfast I might accompany *le patron*'s wife to the market in order to carry back her shopping bags for her. The market was full of startling things to see and hear and smell: cheeses the shape of women's breasts; whole smoked legs of pigs; bunches of mute songbirds with closed eyelids, threaded together by their beaks; live chickens which the man would guillotine for you on request in his special box, the blood running obligingly into the gutter.

For lunch, *madame* knocked up plates of *charcuterie*, tomatoes and lettuce in oil and vinegar, with plenty of *baguette* which I ate at the bar with the customers. For dinner: *potage*, meat or fish and *frîtes*. Soft smelly cheese. Wine and water. Apricots or grapes. I was always hungry and put away whatever was placed in front of me.

Throughout the day different types would drop into the bar for a drink: working men in paint-flecked overalls, shop girls, young couples, elegant women with their wrapped purchases from the *couture* establishments in rue de la Paix. There were no separate private and public areas as there were in pubs in England. Paris, in so many small ways, was different from London. Policemen, sitting at the bar with pistols on their hips, removed their kepis and drank beer like anyone else. If a young woman they knew entered the bar, they would kiss her, drink and share a joke with her, something I found hard to imagine coppers in London ever doing. Men and women kissed each other two or three times whenever they met and again when they said goodbye. When they spoke, the men growled and the women's voices tinkled. The men's hair looked as expensively coiffured as the women's. As in London, everyone smoked and the air was thick with the perfume of women and the acrid aroma of foreign tobacco. In the evening, the gentlemen were dressed in smart suits with wide lapels and ties, the ladies beautifully made up in their pretty, low-cut dresses. One or two would be in evening dress, stopping by for a drink on their way to the opera. Gentlemen came into the bar on their own, sat at the *zinc* talking and smoking, drinking and talking, as Dad and his friends did in the V&A, and then left with the young lady they had met at the bar. I emptied the ashtrays, dried the glasses and stacked them, carried drinks to the tables, as the barman directed me, and played the pinball machines with my tips. My presence in the bar came to be accepted by everyone and a few of the regulars were soon greeting me by name. *Bon soir, monsieur Nill. How you are?* I stayed up until I felt tired enough to go to bed – much later than Mum would have allowed. The jukebox played haunting *chansons*, several of which would stay with me all my life, and around them the emotions I experienced during this period crystallised for ever.

Left to shift for myself, I either hung around the bar, helping out or doing errands, or else I roamed the streets, bored and hungry, exploring the area around the fairy-cake Opéra building, every day venturing further afield. Except for the traffic, which travelled on the wrong side of the road, Paris was a city like London. I did the sort of things I did in London, sauntered in whichever direction the whim took me, stared in shop windows, purchased buns from *boulangeries*, loitered, gawped, slivers of Dylan Thomas crossing my mind: *Grief, thief of time . . . And Death shall have no dominion.* I felt more at home in the street, in the crowd of people ebbing and flowing up and down the *rues* and *boulevards*, than I did in the bar. Strolling incognito among the inhabitants of the city as they hurried about their business, observing, unobserved – *there* and at the same time *not there* – I was a *boulevardier*, a *flâneur*.

Paris, which hadn't been bombed during the War, seemed a lot shabbier than London, which had been. It looked poor and uncared-for and was marvellously smelly. I sauntered the length of avenue de l'Opéra, then up the hill to Montmartre towards the white alabaster Saracen's helmet of le Sacré-Coeur. More often, I strolled the length of rue de la Paix as far as the Jardin des Tuileries and the avenue des Champs-Elysées from where, in the distance, I could see the Eiffel Tower. I enjoyed looking at the Seine, leaning over the embankment and watching the old men in berets who fished in the river, as old men did at the reservoir at Hammersmith, and the laden barges, that followed each other in single file on the water without appearing to move, as one moment follows another.

I liked Paris. I liked the noisy markets where they sold live animals to cook and eat, and the waiters serving at tables outside the expensive bars and restaurants in their dashing uniforms. The elegantly dressed young women on the corner of rue de la Paix and the splendid motor cars that pulled up at the kerb which the young women stepped into. I liked the babble on all sides of a language I didn't speak and so could ignore, which allowed me to pursue my own thoughts. Nobody had any reason to address any words to me, nor I to them. I knew nobody and nobody knew me. I especially liked pissing in the open-air *pissoirs*.

Sometimes I took with me my brother's box camera, which was the kind of camera you looked down into a prism that showed, upside down, a misty version of the image to be captured. The reels of film were on metal spools that you wound by hand by means of a rotating handle. I photographed things that particularly took my fancy: *pissoirs*, barges on the Seine, the Eiffel Tower in the distance, Parisians without their knowledge, like a spy.

But as I kicked around the streets of the 9th *arrondissement*, at a loose end, it wasn't the city that took me by surprise so much as the intensity of my emotions. I found myself periodically ambushed by a feeling of detachment, of my physical separateness from other people. In a sense, this was simply what was the case: I was a foreign body who had no reason to be here; with no connection with any person and no allegiance, I didn't belong. Since nobody could say where I was or what I was doing at any particular moment, because nobody around me, neither the strangers I lived with nor those I passed in the street, gave me a second thought, I roved among the citizens of Paris like a ghost, invisible.

At such times I was subject to a heightened awareness of human mortality. I found myself considering the fact that everyone alive must eventually die, including me, something that had never struck me before. It wasn't the death of any particular individual that impressed me, of my mum or dad, for example, my brother or sister or even me. It wasn't fear. It was more the shocking banal truth that everyone I knew – and everyone I didn't know – was mortal. I felt I had a duty to stop strangers in the street in order to warn them: *Death* shall *have dominion*! Luckily for them I didn't speak their language. One *chanson* frequently played on bar jukeboxes – 'L'Accordéon' sung by a *chanteuse* called Juliette Gréco – had the effect of triggering these bouts of anomie. The tune, each time I heard it, produced in me a *déjà vu*-like sensation: a sudden loss of conviction, like the moment before a moment of nausea.

Later, in the rear of Bar Daunou – in the lull after the afternoon drinkers had departed and before the early evening crowd arrived – I dropped a 10-franc token into the slot in the *billard électrique*. I pulled back the spring mechanism that ejected the steel ball from the chamber into the chute with a satisfying *k-lonk*. I released the mechanism, which instantly cannonaded the ball towards the arena of flashing discs. For a moment, at the perihelion of its trajectory, the ball paused, then meandered slowly down until it came into contact with the charged energy of one of the discs, upon which it rebounded with a percussive *B-bamm!* and then careened into others. *B-bamm! B-bamm!* By means of the two side-flippers and gentle nudges to the table the ball could sometimes be persuaded to confound the pull of gravity and continue to make exciting noises until – *Tilt! Game Over!* – it rolled back into the hole and became inert. I repeated the procedure until my supply of 10-franc tokens was exhausted.

Each evening at seven o'clock sharp I ate soup and bread, steak and chips, with the young barman or *le patron* and his wife, who didn't seem to have children of their own. If they did, I never saw them. My hosts were neither friendly nor unfriendly. They were correct. I did my best to be helpful around the bar, since it was in my interests to ingratiate myself with my hosts, but I wasn't part of their household. I didn't live with them or sleep where they slept – and I never learnt where that was. At night I climbed the stone staircase of the old apartment block to the room with the skylight in the sloping ceiling, where I kept my tortoise in my bed and fed him – or her – salad leaves from my pocket. I didn't object to the slimy stuff that came out of Max's rear, staining the sheets green. I was glad to have a companion. I leafed through the pages of the young barman's cycling magazines, comforted by the hum of the traffic around place de l'Opéra six storeys below. In the airless nights under the hot mansards I lay in bed without pyjamas under a single sheet.

One night, putting aside the cycling magazine, I crept out of my room into the corridor to have a pooh. The toilet cubicle was directly opposite my room, which was handy, if a bit smelly. You had to stand – or, as now, squat – on the ceramic foot-shapes, which might be wet, to do your business. You wiped yourself with squares of a newspaper called *L'Equipe* that hung on a wire. I first pushed the button of the corridor light on the wall to the left of my door, which was on a timer, then quickly nipped into the toilet. With the only light coming through the door ajar, you had to look sharp, to do what you had to do before it turned itself off. But on this occasion, while I was poohing into the hole, I heard a little click out in the corridor: the sound of the snib of a Yale latch slotting into its housing as the door to my room pulled itself to. And then

– I still hadn't finished my pooh – the light of the corridor extinguished itself and I was in the dark. I was locked out of my room. I was squatting bare naked on two ceramic foot-shapes in a French toilet, pooh in my bum-hole.

How – I wondered, wiping myself with the squares of *L'Equipe* – was I going to extract myself from this predicament?

I pressed the dimly glowing button in the corridor and light returned, which only served to illuminate my nakedness. In the end – what else could I do, if I wasn't to stand out in the corridor all night? – I knocked on the door next to my own door. There was no light coming from under it. I didn't know who occupied the room. After a moment, I knocked again. After another moment I heard the murmur of voices. A light came on and a young woman in a silk dressing-gown opened the door and looked at me, astounded to see before her a blond-haired boy, naked, blinking in the light of her room, with his hands in front of his penis.

'*Bonjour madame. Je m'appelle Neil. Je viens d'Angleterre. J'ai dix ans. Comment allez-vous?*'

The woman spoke to me in French and so I didn't understand what she was saying. I explained to her in English that I was from the room next to hers and I was locked out. Behind her I could see her bed, which was to the right of the door, as it was in my own room. There was a man in the bed. The woman scooped me up and, kicking the man out of the bed, laid me in his place, which was deliciously warm. She made the man put his trousers on and go down and fetch the concierge. He was gone about twenty minutes. By the time the concierge had been found and she had brought up a key to my room, the young woman had put a garment on me and was sitting on the bed beside me with her arm around me, chatting to me in

French. After the concierge had opened my door, the young woman led me to my room. She put me to bed and tucked me up. She placed a kiss onto my forehead.

'Bonne nuit, chéri.'

The following evening there was a knock at my door.

'Salut, mon p'tit copain!'

Smiling, my pretty neighbour handed me a white cardboard patisserie box tied with a gold ribbon. She came into my room and sat on my bed beside me.

'Je m'appelle Suzy. Et toi?'

'Je m'appelle Neil.'

'Nill?'

'Oui.'

'Ça va, Nill?'

'Oui. Ça va, Suzy.'

Suzy was enchanted by my tortoise and, while I ate the chocolate gateau she had brought me, she fed Max pieces of lettuce. After Max and I had consumed our treats, she put her arms around me and enveloped me in the warmth of her body.

Suzy was older than my sister and younger than my mother, neither a girl nor a woman. Her skin exuded a powerful, complex fragrance that had the effect of anaesthetising my diffidence, drawing me towards her like an insect into the petals of a flower. She understood how much I wanted her to envelop me in her embrace.

Suzy became my first and only friend in Paris. Each time she saw me afterwards, whenever we passed each other on the stairs, she spoke to me and kissed me on each cheek.

'Salut, mon petit copain anglais! Ça va, Nill?'

'Ça va, Suzy.'

'Alors! Viens ici! Embrasse-moi!'

Sometimes she was with a gentleman but never the same gentleman, never the one she had ordered to put his trousers on and fetch the concierge. I never saw him again. Suzy, who was warm-hearted and pretty, loosened the python-grip the gravelly voiced chanteuse on the jukebox had over my imagination.

Suzy's room, although it had identical dimensions to mine, was much more lived-in and comfortable. She had a dressing table with bottles and lotions, lipsticks and eye make-up and pieces of jewellery; an armchair with a shawl thrown over it, a standing lamp. Several different perfumes jostled against each other and a close, female odour. A green brocade screen stood in front of the washbasin, over which she slung her clothes and behind which she dressed. She had a radio. I made myself comfortable on her bed, the radio quietly relaying romantic *chansons* while she sat in front of her mirror in her slip, brushing her hair and rouging her lips, just as I did at home when my mother was at her dressing table, getting ready to go out. Suzy went out every evening.

One sunny afternoon I took a photograph of Suzy standing on the corner of avenue de l'Opéra. She was wearing a pretty blue and white dress, a broad white belt, heels. She struck a pose for my camera like one of the mannequins in the windows of the *couture* shops in rue de la Paix.

After I had been in Paris about a month or so things began to go downhill at Bar Daunou. *Le patron* and *madame* had become increasingly less correct with me and seemed not to notice whether I was present or not. I could tell they were unhappy about something and I tended to keep out of their way, wandering the streets for long stretches of time, rather than hang around the *zinc*. Because nobody was washing my clothes any more and I often didn't bother to wash myself, my appearance began to deteriorate. Suzy came into the bar one day and spoke about me to *madame*, who shrugged her shoulders without looking at her. Soon after that Jack Grierson – tall, unsmiling, *très* British – appeared in the bar and *le patron* and *madame* exchanged cross words with him in French. Grierson turned to me and exchanged some cross words with me in English. I told him he shouldn't shout at me because he wasn't my father. Jack Grierson slapped my face in front of everyone in the bar, so I whacked him in the belly as hard as I could and got in a couple of good kicks to his shins before I was hauled off. Several customers jumped to my defence, expressing their disapproval to the tall pipe-smoking Englishman who hit children. I had more friends there than he did.

Grierson telephoned England – he gave my father's number, PARk 2674, to the operator. He must have previously booked his call to England, as you needed to do then. I heard him tell my dad that *monsieur* and *madame* were very angry because they had not received the sum of money that had been agreed upon and – quite untruthfully, I thought – that I was behaving badly. He said he was washing his hands of me. I was handed the receiver and Dad spoke to me. He told me – how wonderful it was to hear his voice! – that he was very disappointed with me. I had let him down and I must come home immediately.

Two days later, looking less spruce than I did in my passport photograph, I was on board another BEA Vickers Viscount bound for London, another beautiful air hostess was making a fuss of me, another pilot showed me the controls. Mum and Dad were waiting for me on the far side of Customs. Instead of giving me a good telling off, which was what I had been expecting, they were smiling and laughing and giving me hugs. They seemed pleased to see me. On the drive home they plied me with questions about Paris. Had I seen the Eiffel Tower? Yes. Napoleon's Tomb? No. The Champs Elysées? Yes. I answered their questions without saying anything. My account omitted any mention of Suzy, Juliette Gréco, Max, my intimations of mortality. I already understood that the moment things were put into words they ceased to be true.

Before I left Paris I knocked on Suzy's door. I wanted to give her something and the only thing I had worth giving was my tortoise. I asked Suzy if she would look after Max for me until I came back for him – or her. She said yes, of course she would love to do that. Suzy had learnt to appreciate what a good companion a tortoise can be. Then – she was lying in her bed – she drew me down into her arms and for the last time folded me into the fragrant warmth of her body. She kissed me.

'Au revoir, Nill!'

'Au revoir, Suzy.'

'Re-mem-ber me*! Oui?'*

'Oui.'

Le patron and his wife had not been in the bar to see me off but the young barman was there to shake my hand before delivering me into the care of Jack Grierson, who was waiting outside in his Citroën, smoking his pipe. He thanked me for helping him out and gave me a packet of Hollywood chewing gum for the journey. I was sorry to leave the pinball machines, particularly as neither of them was in use at that moment.

Bam!

B'bam-B'bam! Bam!

Tilt!

Game Over!

The photographs I had taken in Paris with my brother's box camera Dad took into Boots the Chemist to be developed. When they came back, they looked liked this:

Metamorphosis

Dad, having first secured my bicycle to the roof-rack of the Alvis and stowed my kit in the boot, drove me out of West London and up the A40 into Oxfordshire. Once we were in the Chilterns, without consulting the map, he took the first B road he liked the look of. Immediately, we were among silent pastures and meadowland and we knew we were close to our destination. It was a landscape empty of people and traffic. On each side hedged fields followed the gentle up-down contours of the land, the harvest waiting. In England at this time the only vehicles to be met with on country roads tended to belong to people who had business in the country: farm workers or villagers with local purposes, usually agricultural ones. Occasionally, livestock. More than anything, Dad loved to motor through the countryside; to change down into a bend, accelerate out of it, following the line of ancient elms; to bisect the beech coppice that broke up the shaft of sunlight entering through the open sunroof of the Alvis; to be where Sunday drivers need not be taken into account. At a village called Stoke Talmage we stopped at the Red Lion for a spot of lunch. In the bar Dad engaged in conversation a pair of startled locals to whom he explained our purpose and he extracted from them the information he required.

Keep goin' till ye reaches a crassroads. Stay leff an leff agin, then keep on goin' down that lane. Ye can't miss it. Jessup shull sort ye out, fur sure.

He rewarded the two old boys with a brace of half pints.

It was typical of Dad to search for an unknown destination by means of chance encounters and intuition, dispensing with the map. Any bloody fool could follow a map. He preferred to entrust his fate to the aleatory, to leave the beaten track and follow his nose. It was risky to rely on luck but much more fun than executing a carefully laid plan. If you wanted to be lucky, you had to throw the dice; there was no point keeping them in your pocket.

Following his nose, we ended up in a farmyard enclosing ancient pieces of machinery, a tractor, several brown chickens, a black and white dog wagging its tail, the niff of muck. Dad approached the man in muddy boots who had emerged from the barn to see what the big-engined city motor car was doing in his farmyard. *If it's no trouble. Did he have any objection? For a week?* The man – farmer Jessup – had no objection. *S'no trouble. The boy ud be welcome. Ee can come be the house fur milk an eggs an zuch like.* Dad introduced me to Mr Jessup, who shook my hand, showed me where I could draw water, where to leave my bicycle. He nodded towards a stand of elms where I might like to set up camp.

Juss knock at the door, ever you wants summat.

After Dad had executed a three-point turn and driven off back to West London, I shouldered my rucksack and headed in the direction of the field the farmer had indicated. Almost immediately, I was lost.

With the five-pound note Dad had given me for the purpose I had bought a cotton pup tent for two pounds ten shillings in the Army Surplus Store on the Edgware Road, a ground sheet for thirty bob, a set of billycans for 12/6, a sheath knife for 7/6. I had inherited my brother's meths spirit stove and his folding knife, fork and spoon set, his canvas rucksack, his sleeping bag, his thumbed copy of *Scouting for Boys*. But I hadn't inherited his handiness with tools, his height or his knack for getting things right. I had never been a Scout myself and so I knew nothing about how to camp, tie knots, track bears or kill snakes. All I knew was that I was supposed to paint my Swan Vestas with Mum's red nail varnish to keep out the damp, which I had done. I didn't know what a fly-sheet was, nor that it was a good idea to have one. When I pitched my tent, it would be for the first time.

More or less where the farmer had suggested, I set up camp. The field was bounded on one side by an ancient hedge, on another by a copse of ashes sloping down to a quiet little river hidden behind overhanging trees. Old cowpats and fist-sized lumps of rock lay scattered about the shorn grass. The field was pasture that had been grazed and was doing its best to return to meadowland. On the margin of it cow-parsley grew to the height of my elbows. Orange-tips, large brown and small blue butterflies and a froth of tiny moths were busy chasing each other up and down invisible spiral staircases.

After I had succeeded in putting the tent up – grateful no Scoutmaster was present to watch – I arranged my store of provisions: sausages, tins of beans, powdered mashed potatoes, biscuits, tea, bread, Smarties, Tizer. I was already experiencing the best thing about camping: the absence of Other, the sufficiency of Self, the pleasure of being without routine or the voices of authority, radio, the TV. I didn't know yet that the best thing about camping was also the worst.

I collected wood and kindling from the copse. With some of the rocks that lay conveniently to hand, I made a circle for my campfire which I lit with my nail-varnished Swan Vestas. While my sausages were cooking in the frying pan and I was poking them with a fork, happy as Larry, the rocks started to explode like grenades. Shattering, hot splinters spat in all directions. I dived for cover. The rocks were flint. One of the pages of *Scouting for Boys* I had skipped, as I had nearly all of them, must have warned boys that flint is best avoided for this purpose because it is a fissiparous material: subject to fission when heated.

I ate my sausage sandwich and drank my Tizer as the sun went down behind the stand of elms on the crest of the upward gradient. Noisy rooks and jackdaws, first in ragged mobs, then in sixes and sevens, finally in ones and twos, settled onto the uppermost branches of the trees, their murmuration abating as dusk gave way to evening. By slow degrees the world grew dark, then darker still, until the only light was the glow from the embers of my fire and, overhead, the minute glimmerings of innumerable celestial bodies separated from each other by vast distances. The only sounds were of leaves rustling against each other and, now and then, a whoo-whooing that I supposed were owls warning the mice and shrews: *Coming, ready or not!* I crawled into my tent, fastened the opening and by the light of a candle read my book:

> . . . I remember him as if it were yesterday, as he came plodding to the inn door, his sea-chest following behind him in a hand barrow; a tall, strong, heavy, nut-brown man; his tarry pigtail falling over the shoulders of his soiled blue coat . . .

In the stillness outside the tent each discrete sound was amplified: the snap of a twig, the ruffle of feathers, the knock of moths against the outer surface of the canvas. Nearby, some sort of night insect was making an *itch-itch-itching* sound. After a chapter of my book I blew the candle out and, in the suddenly absolute darkness, I jacked off.

Although I had made a few stabs at this solitary activity before, it was in the peace and quiet of the Oxfordshire countryside that I mastered the art. Over the past twelve months startling changes had been taking place in my physiology: hairs had sprouted where previously no hairs had been; the cartilage in my nose had grown so that I had begun to look like someone else: my dad when he was a naval cadet. Waking up in the night with a painfully stiff penis and a stale yoghurt-like fluid over the sheets, a circumstance outside my control, was bewildering. Nobody in my family had thought to warn me that this bizarre occurrence was likely to befall a thirteen-year-old boy. At first I didn't connect it with girls. I soon found out that thinking about girls brought the event on; simply thinking about the event brought it on. It wasn't something I could do anything about. You could get an erection without warning at any time of day or night: doing your maths homework at the kitchen table, waiting for a 49 bus in the rain. It could be very annoying. I knew it had something to do with girls – but what? I had glimpsed my sixteen-year-old sister's breasts through the open armhole of her baby-doll nightdress as she leaned over the sink. Peeping through the hinge-end of her half-closed door, I had seen her in her panties and bra. I had read the folded-down page in the paperback novel she kept under her pillow in which a man, having tied a naked girl to a bed, had smeared her nipples with fresh cream and then – my penis stirring – had licked it off.

Taking advantage of the healthy, open-air life of *Scouting for Boys*, whenever the urge overcame me, I jacked off into squares of white tissue paper.

Each morning, after I woke up, I lolled in my sleeping bag listening to the birds while the sun warmed up the tent. Then I dressed, lit my fire and prepared breakfast, which I ate while I read my book. After I had washed up in boiled river water, emptied my bowels into a hole in the opposite corner of the field and made my camp ship-shape, I completed two pages of my Latin primer. Then I walked to the farmhouse and said good morning to Mrs Jessup, collected my bicycle from the smelly barn and rode it to the little shop in Stoke Talmage to buy provisions: more Smarties, more Tizer. Sometimes Mrs Jessup gave me a slice of something sweet, a pie or a cake. The weather was always fine, gloriously sunny, in fact, and so I didn't have cause to regret not having brought a flysheet. I spent most of my time by the river, lying on the grass reading, watching out for the kingfisher, sharpening the point of my spear with my sheath knife, snoozing.

But more than the kingfisher, it was the dragonflies that caught my eye. The river was neither fast-flowing nor deep and, in the corner of the field nearest to my camp, had been dammed. There the water, shaded by tall ashes and stumpy uncoppiced beeches, collected into a pool that was alive with tiny flying insects and, cruising over the surface, dragonflies eating them. These flashy spivs of the air did not fly with the droll, flapping randomness of butterflies but patrolled their territory in ruthless zig-zags, devouring their prey and sometimes bits of each other, their slender abdomens glinting in the sun. Viridian. Sapphirine. Chrome-yellow. Jet.

According to my copy of *The Observer's Book of Insects*, there were two kinds of dragonfly, hawkers and darters: those that hung stationary over the water like hawks and those that darted over it. *The Golden-Rimmed, the Blue-tailed, the Downy Emerald. The Broad-bodied Chaser, the Black-lined Skimmer, the Ruddy Darter.* There were also the slower, more delicately built, gossamer-winged damselflies: *the Beautiful Demoiselle, the Banded Damsel.* I was intrigued by the phenomenon called metamorphosis. It seemed strange and scary to me that a creature that only a week or so ago had been a sluggish water-bound bug should have been able to transform itself into a shimmering diaphanous flying thing. It was another of those indications, which I had been noticing more and more lately, that the world was both vast and very small. A dragonfly, apparently, spent most of its life submerged as an undistinguished brown grub called a nymph that fed on tadpoles until, in June or July, it crawled up a reed out of the water, emerging from the nymph's exoskeleton as a shiny green or blue dragonfly. These brilliant imagos then darted and hawked to their hearts' content. They started having some fun:

> During mating the male grasps the female by the head or neck while she brings her genital aperture into contact with the sperm capsule on the male's abdomen. The pair then fly off in tandem.

I watched copulating couples, conjoined in their aerial embrace, skimming over the surface of the pool. Nearby, a glistening turquoise male emperor settled onto a waterside plant and remained there, stationary, as if considering which lucky genital aperture should accommodate his sperm capsule.

When the sun became too hot I removed my clothes and lay like a lizard on a patch of hot grass. Being naked in the open air, conscious of the exposure to the world of my penis and scrotum, was a new experience for me, and I let myself imagine that I wasn't alone but was being secretly watched, which I found dangerous and exciting, and immediately my penis began to stir. Before my erection could properly get going I slid into the deliciously cool water like an amphibious reptile and floated just under the surface. The Thing from the Lagoon.

After my swim I walked back across the field towards my tent, the late afternoon sun on my naked body, my penis threatening at any moment to undergo its magical transformation. I was a naked hunter in the bush, alone with my spear.

As well as *The Observer's Book of Insects*, I had with me *Collins British Birds*, a Latin primer called *Civis Romanus Sum*, the *Penguin Selection of Contemporary Verse* and *Treasure Island*. All of these books, except the Latin primer, had my brother's name on the flyleaf in his elegant italic hand. I had recently discovered that reading was one way to get through the empty periods of time I tended to have on my hands. It took my mind off the changes my body was going through. It took my mind off girls. While *Treasure Island* engaged the imagination in a thrilling tussle between Good and Evil, contemporary poetry left me flummoxed. What on earth did these words mean? My understanding of poetry was even more rudimentary than my knowledge of camping.

I had brought with me the school Latin primer *Civis Romanus Sum* because I had set myself the goal of teaching myself Latin over the summer holidays. At the large, brand-new comprehensive school I attended Latin was taught, but only to the A-grade students in the top classes, those who had passed their 11-plus exam. The school accepted children of all abilities, that was the point of a comprehensive school, from the cleverest to the 11-plus failures like me, and those referred to by the letters ESN – educationally sub-normal – and there were fifteen classes, which added up to three hundred pupils in each year. But the classes were streamed – E, D, C, B, A – and it had taken me three years to make my way from the murky lower depths, where the rough diamonds and dimwits were to be found, up towards the bright sparks in the higher reaches. When I returned to school after the summer holiday I would join 4A1, where there were girls who lived in W8 and carried violin cases to school, whose fathers and mothers were doctors and teachers. It was official: I was no longer a dimwit. I had decided to learn Latin because I had been given to understand by my brother, who had Latin *and* Greek, that a person could not properly call himself educated who did not have it. I never questioned anything my brother told me. I took his pronouncements as gospel.

Each day I studied two pages of my primer and completed the exercises, jotting down and memorising the cases of nouns and adjectives, the declensions of verbs, word order. Applying myself to the task methodically, without being coerced, I found the challenge fun and I aimed to complete in ten weeks the work the Latin class had taken two years to cover. I had already studied Italian for two years and so this was not so difficult as it sounds. By September I had to be ready for the O level set text: *Caesar's Gallic Wars Book I.* Nouns after prepositions of place take the nominative case; things and people addressed, the vocative; verbs following verbs of fearing, the subjunctive. Latin was complicated but it was knowable. Compared to the poems in the Penguin collection, it was straightforward.

One morning I was working in my notebook while my bacon sizzled in the frying pan when, glancing up, I noticed a person on the far edge of the field, standing beneath an elm. I didn't know how long he had been standing there, watching me. I pretended I hadn't seen him. I returned to my notebook. Next time I looked towards the elm, the person had gone. Was that a good or a bad thing? On the occasion the farmer had visited me with his dog, he had walked straight up to my tent and asked me if everything were all right. But I didn't know who this fellow was nor what he wanted. The next time I looked up he was standing a few yards from me: a big-boned, straw-haired fellow wearing a flat cap.

''Ello,' he said.

'Hello.'

'You campin' 'ere, then?'

'Yes.'

'Yur cookin yur breakfast, I see.'

'Yes.'

'What you cookin'?'

'Egg and bacon.'

'Mm. Smells good.'

He didn't introduce himself to me. I didn't know how to introduce myself to him. I wasn't frightened. I didn't have the sense to be frightened. I had met boys like him at school. I wondered whether he might not be a bit ESN.

'Where you fram, then?'

'London.'

'*Lunnon?*'

He sounded surprised that a person could come from so remote and exotic a place.

'Yes.'

'I niver bin to Lunnon. What you writin'?'

I wasn't writing. I was making a coloured pencil drawing of a dragonfly from one of the photographs in *The Observer's*

Book of Insects. It wasn't very good. I showed my sketch to the young man who had never been to Lunnon.

'That's good!' he said, sounding as if he meant it.

Neither of us could think where the conversation should go from here and so, after a moment, my visitor said, 'Well, I bess be goin'. Joy yur bacon an' egg.'

It was during this week on my own in the bush, away from civilisation, that I first tried my hand at writing. I don't know why. In the company of my elders and betters I should never have presumed to take myself so seriously. I started to write because I was alone and I had nothing better to do, like everybody else.

At some level I must have understood that this camping business, this Latin-learning and poetry reading, was an imposture. I wasn't following my own inclinations; I was following my brother's. I was daring myself to be like him.

Having struggled through so many poems I couldn't make head nor tail of, I decided to write one I could understand:

THE NYMPH

The nymph that lurked
yesterday in the slurry
at the bottom of the pond

today is drawn towards the light
of the sun floating
on the surface of the water.

Leaving herself behind,
she darts across the sky
on invisible wings.

It wasn't much of a poem, even I could see that. Some of the words I had filched from my *Observer's Book of Insects*. And if it meant anything, what did it mean?

But I was pleased enough with it to copy out different versions onto squares of white paper. This was my first poem.

I had long come to the conclusion that words were not to be relied on. If I had learnt anything in the Church Army Home for Motherless Children it had been this. Since the meanings of words are fixed by other people, it would be unwise to put your trust in them when communicating private information to the world at large. To convey the personal you needed to be oblique, sly and devious, careful not to put your meaning into words, like a spy speaking a foreign tongue in enemy territory. You had to be on your guard in order not to betray yourself, because if you did, if you made a false move, you would be found out and unmasked as an impostor.

Writing, like jacking off, was an activity that didn't require the participation of another person. Done alone, in secret even – what was there to be gained by discussing it with a third party? It was a guilty pleasure best kept quiet about.

I never saw my visitor again, although I sometimes sensed that he was not far away. I knew he had paid visits to my camp in my absence because one morning, on my return from the village, I had found a large white egg, a duck egg, sitting in my frying pan. On another occasion, the undamaged shiny fluorescent-blue carcass of an emperor dragonfly resting on my notebook.

At the end of seven days I struck camp and packed my gear into my rucksack. Dad arrived before lunch. He thanked Mr Jessup for letting me camp on his land. He tried to press paper money on him in payment for the milk and hospitality I had received but Farmer Jessup wasn't having it. Mrs Jessup gave me a slice of something sweet for the journey. While they talked, I stowed my stuff into the boot of the Alvis and roped my bicycle onto the roof-rack, and then Dad drove us back up the A40 to London. On the way home he quizzed me about my week. How had it gone? Had it been difficult to be on my own? No, it hadn't been difficult. It had been fine. I told him about the exploding flint stones and about the kingfisher. I told him I had read *Treasure Island*, a seafaring adventure story for boys by a Scottish author, one of his favourite books.

I didn't tell him what I had found out, something I hadn't known before the week I had spent under the stars, a native boy alone in the bush with his spear, unsupervised by his elders and betters. I was going to be a writer.

Betrayed

The first girl whose lips I kissed was Charlotte David of form 4A2, in the place we and our friends used on Saturday nights for our parties, the unoccupied attic room on top of Debbie Clarke's flat over the National Provincial Bank in Notting Hill Gate. At these events the lights were dimmed in order to conceal which lips were kissed, whose hands touched. We were groping in the dark. Either Chris Montez was singing 'Let's Dance' or the Ronettes 'Be My Baby' on Debbie's beat-up Dansette record-player. We only had a handful of 45 rpm records: The Beatles: 'Please Please Me'; the Crystals: 'He's A Rebel'; Buddy Holly: 'That'll Be The Day'. Almost everyone at these parties was from the same classes at school: those embarking on their GCE O level courses. We were all just as clever as each other but because of the type of school it was we came from very different social backgrounds: Kensington Square W8, Southam Street W10, the Worlds End Estate SW17, the foreign embassies around Kensington Gore. In my class the previous year, 3B2, Sandra Crick, whose dad ran Crick's, the greengrocer on Kensington Church Street, sat next to an American girl called Anjelica Huston, who had returned to California at the end of the year.

Holland Park Comprehensive – a modern light-filled campus on Campden Hill next to the park, an expression of postwar optimism by the London County Council that had opened for business just when I needed it – had tennis courts, a swimming pool, spanking new labs, a theatre with flies and lights and a pit for the orchestra. Music practice rooms, a kiln, engineering and carpentry workshops. In the sunny art rooms at the top of the East Block you could observe peacocks on the uppermost branches of the trees in the park and, while you painted, hear them squawking. Three basketball courts. Finally, the cards had begun to fall my way. As a first-year soprano on Inauguration Day I had sung 'Jesu Joy Of Man's Desiring' before the new head boy welcomed His Worship the Mayor. The new head boy – tall, good-looking, captain of the First XV, victor ludorum, wearing a scarlet waistcoat with gold buttons under his blazer and Head Prefect badge – had been my brother. Now, four years later, the school basked in the prestige of appearing in the pages of the *Mail* and the *Express*, outraged by our cocky co-ed egalitarianism. The children of senior Labour politicians had not left their expensive public schools to join us yet, but they would do soon, once their dads saw which way the wind was blowing. Holland Park was new and fashionable; even posh parents wanted their kids to go there. I knew a girl from St Paul's Girls School who bunked in for a day without any of the teachers even noticing she was there.

I thought Charlotte was pretty but *she* didn't. She compared herself to other girls who looked older, were more developed and who, she thought, had something she didn't. As I held her in my arms, my hand against the fabric covering her extraordinarily thin body, the small of her back, the strap of her trainer bra, I felt I was recovering something I had hidden long before. I was intrigued by everything about her: her cheap Woolworth's perfume, her long black hair that she ironed on an ironing-board and sometimes tucked into the neck of her black top. She nearly always wore black clothes: black sweaters, little black skirts, smoky black tights. Finally girls in London had started to dress like Juliette Gréco. We were fifteen.

Charlotte and I hung around together. I waited for her in the morning outside her flat in Colville Square and walked her to school and home afterwards. We held hands. Occasionally, we kissed. At weekends we did things together. In school we hardly acknowledged each other because different rules applied there, although we wrote each other *billets-doux* which we passed to each other in the corridor.

Hello, Sweet Boy!
Cheer up! It's not as bad as all that!
Do you really, really, really like me?
Will you be in the Coffee Mill after school?

xxxx Charley

Charlotte was the daughter of a trade union activist who had fought the Fascists during the Notting Hill race riots. He had fought the West Indian henchmen of the slum landlord Peter Rachman and against Sir Oswald Mosley, who had been the Union Movement candidate for Kensington North in the previous election – so she held some strong views about the world. With half a dozen friends we met the CND marchers from Aldermaston at Hammersmith and marched with them to Trafalgar Square behind the Royal College of Music trad jazz band. We wore black and white Anti-Apartheid badges on our lapels and refused to eat South African fruit.

With Charlotte and a boy named Adam Kravitz I attended a demonstration organised by the Committee of 100 against the state visit to London of Queen Frederica of Greece, an ex-Nazi Party member and aunt to Prince Philip. We booed her and obstructed the approach of her Rolls-Royce to Claridge's. Eggs were thrown. I ran the wrong way and I was collared, arrested and tossed into the meat-wagon and taken to Cannon Street police station where I was held until Dad arrived to bail me. While I was in the police station my fingers found the two fireworks in my pockets Adam Kravitz had given me to look after for him.

At Horseferry Road Magistrates' Court the next morning Dad paid my £2 fine and then took me to a pub for lunch. He made no adverse comment about my arrest. He took the view that it's the job of young people to express their contempt for the decisions of their elders and betters. As for being nabbed by the Law, that was one of the hazards a chap ran in life. I had learnt a valuable lesson.

But, as things turned out, these legal proceedings proved to be one of the events that encouraged us to believe that the times they were a-changin': the first one now would later be last; the order was rapidly changing. The sixties were going to be different. The High Court sent two Cannon Street police officers to prison and one, DS Harry Challenor, to the loony-bin, for fabricating evidence in the case of two of the accused. The police, who had been caught planting bricks in the pockets of innocent demonstrators, had missed the bangers in mine.

Charlotte directed my attention towards the world. She took me to see interesting buildings before they were pulled down. We saw Marlon Brando in *On the Waterfront* at the Electric cinema in Portobello Road. She lent me her copy of *The Catcher in the Rye*. We listened to *The Freewheelin' Bob Dylan*. She knew about the Pyramids, F. Scott Fitzgerald, Martin Luther King. Charlotte taught me things; for example, what a girl's monthly period was. She was not like other girls but her low self-esteem meant that she needed the continual reassurance from other girls that she was. In the end, my devotion was not enough for her. There were too many other taller, more glamorous boys at the parties we went to and – she said – it was easier to deal with their one-tracked minds than the intensity of my emotions. She was under the impression that my mind was less one-tracked than theirs. At a party in Craven Hill Gardens – which intersected my old stamping ground, Gloucester Terrace – she succumbed to the advances of Adam Kravitz, who was generally considered to be a bad lot. She let him kiss her, his arms holding her close to his body, crushing her against his desire, and I walked home alone, desolate. She wrote me a letter to say how really, really, *really* sorry she was, and that we could still be friends. I felt betrayed. My reaction to losing Charlotte was completely out of proportion – even I could see that.

So when Dad said he had a spot of business to do in Scotland that would involve driving up there, staying in the Highlands for a couple of days and then driving back down, and why didn't I join him, I said all right, why not? I didn't particularly feel like going to school, seeing Charlotte or Adam Kravitz or any of my friends. It wasn't a situation I wanted to face but to run away from.

Dad didn't tell me what his spot of business involved and I didn't ask him. It didn't occur to me to ask, any more than he would have thought to pry into my business. My dad and my mum knew nothing about my private life, how I spent my time, who my friends were. They had never met Charlotte. They didn't care what I did in my spare time any more than I cared what they did in theirs. Our lives barely touched. Mum toiled and cooked and grew older. Dad, who was old already, did what he had always done: motored around London in a black and maroon 3-litre Alvis saloon, meeting chaps in pubs, scouting for business, drawing into the night at his board, ever optimistic that one of his ideas was about to take off. My brother was at Oxford. My sister had discovered the existence of handsome American enlisted men at the US forces PX hotel on Bayswater Road. Her unfinished letters to these young GIs, which I perused while she was out of the house, were graphic accounts of how far she had gone with them. She had gone further than I, in my imagination, had thought it possible to go. I got a hard on reading them. She had discovered what she had been stalking all these years: sex. I came home from school, did my homework, ate my meals, slept, left for school, without revealing to the people I lived with the turbid state of my emotions. I felt like a secret agent, careful not to be tricked into making a false move that would reveal who he really was. Disguised as a monosyllabic teenager, I gave no outward indication of my inner life, which was more interesting to me than the lives of the other members of my family. The important thing was that I didn't betray myself to these alien people. The letter in Charlotte's familiar loopy hand on fragrant pale green tissue paper in my pocket had been smuggled across a border:

> Dearest Neil
>
> Why, oh why do you do this to me? I don't know how to treat you except I know I'm nasty to you. I'm sorry I went with Adam on Friday. I can't help it! To my friends I despair of you ever becoming a real glamour boy but when I'm alone there's only one boy I miss and that's you. And you'll never know it. You don't believe me when I say how much I like you. It can't be love. If I loved you, I wouldn't want

to go with other boys. Why do you like me like you do? What is there in me, Neil? I can't understand it. I'm rather plain when you think about it. I say silly things. I'm soppy. I'm terrible at languages. I'm selfish and cruel. One day I'll feel sort of honoured that such a decent boy like you should actually have liked me. I was awfully worried about you when you were arrested. I thought the police would bash you around.

But I'm not apologising for anything. I am this person, not the person you think I am. But I've always dreaded the day we had an argument in case you went off with someone else and I would lose you for ever. But when I came home and found the chain I gave you in an envelope I cried and cried. When I see you, please, please talk to me! Don't pretend you don't know I'm there. Please don't hate me, dearest boy.

xxxxxxxxxxxx Charley

Dad and I drove out of London north-west towards Oxford on the A40, although not exclusively. While it exasperated him to be stuck behind a Ford Popular he couldn't overtake on a single-lane B road, he refused to sit with his foot down on a featureless dual-carriageway. He liked a road that followed the contours of the land, climbing and descending ancient field boundaries. Like Mr Toad – to whom, in many respects, he bore an uncanny resemblance – he sought the freedom of the open road, which gave him the opportunity to use his gears in preference to his brakes when going into a bend. He was temperamentally unable to resist the allure of the picturesque long way round in preference to the more direct common-sense route, in driving as in all things. Dad despised common sense, which he considered to be overrated. No invention had ever come about through the application of common sense. It evoked for him the values of suburban 'Safety First' Baldwin-voting Nazi-appeasing *Daily Express*-reading lower-middle-class types – a description he applied to most people he knew, including members of his own family.

The map was spread out on my knees so that I could read out directions when he sensed a more interesting, Ford Popular-free route. Dad was in excellent spirits. It was easy to be with him in circumstances such as these. While we were alone like this he spoke to me as if we were equals, without condescension. He talked and I listened. I was a handy audience. For long periods, however, while I was looking out of the passenger window or listening to Dad, what I was really doing was thinking about Charlotte. What was she doing now? Who was she thinking about? How would she construe my absence? Would I ever kiss her again? I was learning that the interior life runs its course however a person outwardly seems. I was able to be alert to Dad's interesting observations about the places we were passing through while at the same time surgically recalling to the mind's eye the image of Adam Kravitz kissing Charlotte across the room at David Meyer's party in Craven Hill Gardens, to feel again – and again – that stab into the heart.

By lunchtime we were in Worcester. Dad parked the Alvis in the Cathedral Close and led the way into the gloomy nave. He had been here before. In the north cloister he paused in front of a stained-glass window and directed my attention to the names of his brothers Ian and Duncan inscribed on the glass under the King's School motto, *Regia Schola Wigorniensis*, along with the names of eighty-two other old boys of King's

School – the oarsmen, the batsmen and bowlers, the backs and the forwards, the choristers, the scholars, the clever clogs and the slow-witted – who had fallen with them in the Great War for Civilisation.

After lunch we continued our journey north.

'September 1939, when war was declared, I had just arrived in London from Liverpool with your mother. I needed a job. I began to nose around the East End; Clerkenwell, Plaistow, Hoxton – districts where, in those days, you could find bespoke garages, small precision-tool businesses, specialist engineers. It was there I ran into a sapper major called Millis Jefferies. He was doing the same as me, only from the other end of the production process: on the lookout for engineers. Millis Jefferies – who, I later found out, was a first-class engineer himself – was director of MD1. We got talking. A couple of days later he sent for me. Set me to work on an underwater magnetic mine, which didn't come to anything. It was a cod project to see if I cut the mustard. I must have done because he took me on . . .

'MD1 – sometimes called Winston's Toyshop – worked in Portland Place, in a basement cluttered with lathes and instruments. When that took a direct hit in August 1940, we decamped to a country house called The Firs at Whitchurch in Buckinghamshire, which the MOD had requisitioned. Not quite Brideshead, more the size of the Pirn. Your mother and I and our cat, Herr Shnickelgruber, put up in the grounds in a caravan eighteen feet by five. We lived there until the summer of 1942.

'I was a design draughtsman, one of a small team of clever buggers and, believe me, we worked our socks off! A fourteen-hour day was normal. I didn't realise it at the time but I have never worked so hard in my life, nor been happier, than I was then. I was living with a lovely slip of a girl in a caravan, engaged in Top Secret work, designing weapons to kill the enemy. I could hardly believe my luck. At the ripe old age of thirty-eight I had found a woman who was prepared to put up with me. The set-up was pretty basic. We had no facilities in the caravan, of course. If your mother wanted a bath or a pee she had to use one of the bathrooms in the house – *and* take her own soap. She opened the door of a bathroom one morning to find the PM sitting on the pan, reading. He didn't look up or say a word but June, poor girl, nearly wet herself on the spot!

'It was in that caravan, by the way, that your brother was conceived . . .'

'That must be why he's so clever.'

'Quite possibly.'

'It was while I was at Whitchurch that Millis Jefferies and I dreamed up what later became known as the Hedgehog Bomb. If a salvo of explosive projectiles could be fired *ahead* of a ship attacking a submarine, they would counteract the time-lag involved in carrying out an asdic-directed depth-charge attack. I put this to him while we were strolling over the lawns of The Firs one afternoon in autumn 1940. As we walked, using the fir cones that were lying about, I demonstrated to him what I had in mind. Why couldn't Millis Jefferies's new spigot mortar be adapted as an anti-submarine device on the bow of a fighting ship? A brilliant Canadian chap called Goodeve later worked out how to do it.

'I was also commuting to ICI at Witton in Birmingham, where Fred Lindemann had put a team together. I was set to work on a beam defence system for the new Sterling bomber. I also set up a welding-line to manufacture the P.14 rifle. That kept me busy until summer 1942, when your mother and I took a week's holiday in London. She was seven months pregnant by then.

'By this time I knew that the bloody Navy was never going to give me a commission. I was a damned fool to think it would. As a precaution, I had enlisted as an ordinary seaman under the name of Grant. I was forty by then, doing essential war work, so it wasn't as if I was going to get called up. My papers came through in November 1942, two months after your brother was born, and off I went as an hostilities-only ordinary seaman. I was given basic training and had the rest of my teeth pulled. Then I was sent to Whale Island where they had a gunnery school in a stone frigate, HMS *Excellent*, because I could do the trig. I could to the trig standing on my head . . .'

'Why didn't the Navy give you a commission,' I asked him, 'if you had been to Dartmouth?'

My question was disingenuous. I knew perfectly well, having been enlightened by my sister, why this ex-midshipman had been refused a commission in His Majesty's Navy: because he was an ex-jailbird, he had done six months in His Majesty's chokey. I knew this although Dad had never told me, just as he had never told me he had had a son with Foxie, the woman in Crowborough who had telegrammed him to say she intended to take her own life rather than have a child out of wedlock and it was out of desperation, to prevent this, that he had stolen the car in Exeter. He couldn't marry Foxie, even if he had wanted to, because he was already married, having returned from Canada, at the age of twenty-one, with a wife who was carrying his baby. Dad had named his first son Ian and his second, Foxie's son, Duncan. His first wife was called May and the name he used for our mum was June.

'The Admiralty had its reasons. I should have known better. It was bloody stupid of me. The biggest mistake of my life and, as you know, I've made my share. Your mother never got over it. She was left alone in the Blitz with a new baby on her lap. I was a damn fool. I should have stayed at Whitchurch, knocking out ideas with the brightest engineers in the country. I should have done what I enjoyed doing and was good at. Instead, I spent the rest of the War below deck on various warships, first on the Russian Run from Liverpool to Kola Inlet, then on the Western Approaches. The North Atlantic in winter, you can't imagine what it was like. It was a dreadful experience for me, at the age of forty. Absolute bloody hell. Made me ill . . .'

We crossed into Cumberland towards teatime. Tidy hedged fields had given way to uncultivated uplands. The sky, which until then had been clear, was becoming overcast and Dad asked me to look up in the AA handbook the nearest recommended three-star hotel. As well as the handbook, he had the AA badge on the front bumper and he acknowledged the salute of the patrolman, who wasn't to know his membership had lapsed.

The public house with accommodation appeared on the road into Penrith, just as Dad had assured me it would do. Wherever you travelled with Dad he gave the impression that he had been there before. He was the person it had all been laid on for. His patrician air and antebellum charm opened the door before he pushed against it. We were soon standing in the carpeted lounge bar of the hotel awaiting the dinner gong, half pints of bitter in our hands, Dad entertaining the barman with the story of how his brother, Duncan, returning to Innerleithen from Peebles on his Rudge-Whitworth motorcycle one Christmas Eve before the War, had run out of petrol and had completed the journey by emptying into the tank a bottle of 75% proof whisky. The barman looked sceptical. He hadn't grasped that when Dad said *before the War*, he meant *before the Great War for Civilisation*.

I understood, and partly shared, the barman's scepticism. But to be sceptical of Dad's anecdotes and yarns was to miss the point. His first-person stories were marvellously vivid and stranger than fact. He understood that narrative needs to be more than merely plausible; it must have some magical factor that drops the jaw of the listener. In storytelling, it's not the truth of the story that matters but that it has the ring of truth. Dad's stories rang true because of the amount of canny corroborative detail he gave them.

'You have to remember, dear boy, the size of cylinder-heads in those days. Bloody great things. Had to be, the petrol was of such poor quality . . .'

The next morning we headed for the border. At Moffat, instead of taking the middle course between Glasgow and Edinburgh, such as drivers of Ford Populars and wretched lower-middle-class types with common sense would have done, and as I had suggested myself, we headed north-west towards the Clyde, which we crossed at Erskine to Dumbarton in Argyllshire, heading for Loch Lomond and the Highlands. Finally, after the years of kilts and sporrans, Burns Nights and haggis and first footing, I was in Scotland. The place my dad had talked about throughout my childhood I was finally about to see for myself.

But he still hadn't revealed the purpose of our visit. Why, for example, did we have fishing tackle in the boot of the car? All I knew, as the map-reader, was that our destination was Fort Augustus in Inverness-shire.

'. . . In the fag end of '43 I joined HMS *Magpie*, part of Second Escort Group, which was a squadron of five frigates under a first-rate seaman, F. J. 'Johnny' Walker. I saw Walker several times, but, as a rating, I never met him. It was probably just as well. It might have been awkward. Like him, my first posting after Dartmouth had been midshipman on *Ajax* in the Aegean – he in 1914, I five years later. We had probably slept in the same berth.

'February the second we sailed out of Liverpool, as pretty a flock of frigates as you ever saw. Each of Walker's ships had an ornithological name – *Starling*, *Kite*, *Woodpecker*, *Wild Goose*, Walker's own ship, and *Magpie*. Our mission was to rendezvous with the incoming convoy of merchantmen from the United States and escort them through the Western Approaches, into the range of the U-boat wolf packs.

'Walker had developed his own strategy for attacking submarines. He used two ships to stalk the quarry once the asdic had picked it up. Asdic is a form of sonar, a transmitted sound-beam that bounces back off any submerged vessel, as audible to the submarine's telegraphist on his hydrophone as it is to your own. The way Walker attacked submarines was masterly. One ship got an asdic fix astern of the enemy vessel while the other steamed at about five knots with her asdic silent but following surface signals from the directing ship until she was right over the quarry. The U-boat commander could hear on his hydrophone the pinging of the asdic ship, which gave him a false sense of security since he knew he was out of range of her depth charges. He would have no idea he was about to be attacked. The second ship, when she was exactly where the first ship signalled she should be, released her weapons.

'On the morning of the ninth U-boats were reported to be in the area. Walker didn't wait to be attacked; he went after them. That was his way. *Starling* and *Woodpecker* sank *U762* and then *Wild Goose* destroyed *U743*. *Magpie* was working with *Kite* to the south of the convoy when Walker signalled that the enemy was heading our way and we should engage.

'It's a marvellous thing, you know, to be on a man-o'-war preparing for a sea battle. On deck, the officers, the gun crews and depth chargers; below, the navigators, signallers and engineers, every sailor at his station, Cook dishing out tea and sausage butties. It doesn't come to every man to have the opportunity to strike a mortal blow at the enemy. Perhaps it *was* stupid of me to have enlisted and the sensible thing for me to have done would have been to stay at my drawing board, with your mother and her new baby and Herr Shnickelgruber. The sensible thing would have been to have left the fighting to somebody else. But I can't say I regret being there that day, rangefinder for a 4-incher about to engage the enemy at sea.

'At about forenoon watch *Magpie* got an asdic fix and we tracked the U-boat while *Kite* laid down her depth charges.

She did this through noon until First Dog. No joy. The blighter was still here, going down as deep as she dared. Eventually *Kite* began to run out of ammunition and so we switched roles. It was now about four in the afternoon. We'd been at it for seven hours. The men were all in. I know I was!

'*Magpie* crept over the U-boat dead slow and, at the signal from *Kite*, laid down her depth charges. I was there to witness the firing of Goodeve's Hedgehog mortars, which I like to take some small credit for dreaming up. That was a sight! The ship rocked as the explosions detonated around us and then there was a bloody great bang. We'd got the bugger! We knew we had because *Kite* signalled that the asdic echo had fallen silent. Circling back round, the evidence was all over the water: pieces of gear, oil, clothing, human remains. It was a gruesome sight but a bloody great cheer went up from the men. We'd made our first kill! *U238* wouldn't be sending any more unarmed merchantmen to their deaths.

'From *Wild Goose* Walker sent all ships the signal: *Splice the main brace!* – a double rum ration to all hands!

'Three U-boats had been sunk by Walker's group in the space of twenty-seven hours. When *Starling* and *Wild Goose* and *Magpie* berthed in Liverpool on the twenty-fifth we received a tremendous Navy welcome. Sailors, WRNS, fitters, all turned out along Gladstone dock, waving and cheering. A band played Walker's signature tune, "A-Hunting We Will Go". No *Magpie* sailor had to buy his beer that night, you can take my word for it!'

In the Highlands we were in a foreign country. On either side of the Alvis, hills concertinaed upwards towards ever bigger hills, becoming small mountains in the distance. The country was like a tweedy, tartany piece of fabric that had been tossed up and left crumpled on the ground. We motored north until we reached Fort William. From the window of the expensive white hotel, into which our bags were carried for us, we could see Ben Nevis rising into the mist. Dad tipped the porter with paper money. It hadn't escaped me that he had plenty of cash in his wallet. Dad – as far as I knew, he was unemployed – was getting rid of pound notes as if the sight of them offended him. Once he was in possession of ready cash, the last thing he considered doing with it was putting it in the bank or using it to pay off his creditors. If the stuff was in his pocket, he wanted to spend it as soon as possible, before anyone else got his hands on it.

In the late afternoon we drove into the hills on the lookout for a wee burn where we could try out the rods. We came upon a wee loch, a rowing boat moored against a little wooden jetty, the oars conveniently laid flat on the planks. Dad didn't hesitate. He set the oars in the rowlocks, ordered me aboard, pushed off and rowed out into the open water. I was being given a crash course in how to steal a boat, handle a pair of oars and cast a fly. The part of me that took after Dad thought it was terrifically exciting. The other part of me, the lower-middle-class part that took after my mum, was convinced we would be caught and get into trouble. When you were with Dad you never knew what was going to happen next, and you didn't care – because he didn't. He didn't give a damn. For an engineer, he gave surprisingly little consideration to the consequences his actions were likely to have. It was either alarming or marvellous fun – or, as now, both.

While I fished, Dad took photographs with his new camera.

Over the following couple of days I stood bare-legged in the icy water, my weight straining against the line, fishing for the approval of my dad, who lay on the bank reading the newspaper or snoozing under it – or taking photographs. Dad had with him an expensive new camera – an SLR Pentax. In itself this was no surprise. One of the ways he spent his money, when he had it, was on mechanical toys that took his fancy – tape-recorders, army surplus walkie-talkies, electric card-shuffling machines. But this camera was not his. It belonged to the person from whom he had borrowed the fishing tackle and whose pound notes he was spending. With the Pentax he photographed me casting off or landing some wretched trout. I look a bit wooden in these photographs because my heart wasn't in it. I had never had any desire to fish and nor, as far as I knew, had Dad.

We drove to the furthest end of Loch Oich, tiny in comparison with its famous neighbour, Loch Ness, and booked into a hotel in Fort Augustus and parked our luggage. Then, doubling back on ourselves, we took the small B road, hidden among the spruces, on the opposite bank to the Inverness road we had come by, on which the traffic was non-existent. So it was all the more surprising, after descending on foot from the road down the steep slope to the loch, to chance upon an entire film crew camped out on the shore: vans, cameras on tripods, lights boosting the leaden air, a generator, frogmen chatting to girls with clipboards, all of them smoking cigarettes. The little strand sounded with south-of-the-border voices, cockney ones, mostly.

A man in a sheepskin jacket greeted Dad and they shook hands. I was introduced to this person, whose name I didn't need to be told, having seen him dozens of times on TV. Jonathan Routh routinely gulled innocent members of the public, luring them into taking part in silly or compromising situations. His programme was called *Candid Camera*.

While they conferred with the director, I latched on to the

woman who was handing out sandwiches and coffee which you didn't have to pay for. In due course Dad got the fishing rods from the car and I was positioned on a rock with the line in the water while Mr Routh took photographs with the Pentax. At a signal from the director, a fabulous sea-beast hove into view, manoeuvred by the frogmen in the water underneath it. Looping in and out of the loch as Nessie does in the *Beano*, the monster didn't look at all monstrous but rather too believable to be true. I was photographed as if it just happened to be passing behind me while I was fishing. The careful staging of this extraordinary chance event was done with great earnestness. Nobody was laughing or, it seemed to me, having much fun. It was a job of work being carried out at the union rate.

This, then, was the reason for our trip. Dad had replied to the box-number of a No Questions Asked small ad in *The Times* and, of course, he fitted the bill perfectly. He wasn't only a plausible con artist, he was a plausible Scottish con artist. We were involved in an elaborate hoax hatched in London: the Loch Ness Monster was about to be sighted in Loch Oich by a father and son touring the highlands on a fishing holiday. A film about the set-up would be transmitted after the story broke.

The crew milled and bumped into each other. The light was going. Time was running out. Tempers were fraying. Dad alone seemed to have the measure of the occasion. In his Gieves & Hawkes blazer, Dartmouth cravat and a pin of the Order of St Catherine (Third Class) in his lapel, he looked like the famous actor, Luke Ferguson. Nonchalant in front of the camera, he was in his element, having been paid a couple of hundred quid in cash to do something he would have been happy to do for nothing: drive around the Highlands in a big car, acting like a toff, beguiling people. David Niven couldn't have given a more convincing performance.

Later that afternoon, leaving me in the car – obviously, he didn't want anyone quizzing me – Dad took the undeveloped film into the *Daily Express* office in Inverness and spun them a yarn. He chose the *Express* because it was the newspaper of the sensible, lower-middle-class types he so despised. On Saturday morning the Scottish edition carried pictures of Dad and me and the monster on the front page:

LOCH NESS MONSTER IN LOCH OICH

The question mark conveyed the sub-editor's scepticism. In the photographs the monster looked stagy and unconvincing; Dad, too good to be true. The way they wrote up the story, it wasn't obvious to me who – *whom*, Dad preferred – the joke was on:

> To judge from some remarkable photographs taken just two days ago, the Lock Ness Monster has moved. Or if it hasn't moved, it has a rival tourist attraction in the loch next door – Loch Oich.
>
> Consider the photographic evidence. And then study what the photographer, 60-year-old Mr William Ferguson, a consultant design engineer from Hammersmith, London, has to say:
>
> 'I am on a fishing holiday with my son, Neil. We stopped at Loch Oich at between 4.30 and 5 p.m. on Thursday. We both had a few casts, none of which were successful.
>
> 'My son was casting out again when I happened to glance over my shoulder and I saw this thing on the loch. It was a browny-olive colour – that's as far as I can describe it. Maybe a khaki-olive colour.
>
> 'I waded to the bank and ran to get my camera. It must have taken about 60 seconds to do that. When I first saw the thing it was about 30 yards off shore,

but by the time I got my camera and returned to the water's edge it was further away. I am not sure just how far but possibly twice that distance.

'I took one or two shots but in my excitement couldn't find the object through the viewfinder. The contours of this thing were rather like humps, of which there were two, and sometimes three, above the surface.

'There was a wash behind it. As a former Navy man I estimate that the thing's dimensions would be about 15 to 20 feet. It was travelling at about three to four knots. Definitely not quickly.

'As it moved, it went up and down in the water and finally crossed towards the other side of the loch before disappearing.

'I don't know how long all this took. It was certainly a matter of minutes or seemed so.'

Loch Oich is six miles from Loch Ness, going south-west. If the thing Mr Ferguson saw yesterday was a fugitive from the stretch of water recently, it would have had to negotiate seven lock gates of the Caledonian Canal, swim down past the main street to Fort Augustus and under the noses of seven lock-keepers. The lock-keepers swear no monsters have swum along their way recently.

Mr S. A. Barnett, senior lecturer in zoology at Glasgow University, examined the photographs yesterday and said cautiously: 'The Loch Ness Monster, if one exists, would be a plesiosaur. It has a long, slimy neck with which it reaches out to grab its food.'

He tapped the pictures.

'This beast here does not have such physical characteristics. The second difference is this appearance of heavily armoured scales on the humps. This, too, is at odds with such evidence that we have at the moment. I don't know of any creature, ancient or modern, that looks like this.

'If this were genuine, it would be very exciting but it is essential to know much more about the circumstances.'

> Then he pointed out the pneumatic appearance of the humps.
>
> 'This, too, is not in line with the generally accepted idea of the Monster. If this is a fake, then it has been extraordinarily well done.'

Dad didn't care how seriously the hoax was taken. He had done his job. He had been paid to motor through the Highlands and stay in the best hotels. He felt particularly pleased with himself at having extracted from the despised *Daily Express* a handy bundle of fivers on his own account for the use of his story and photographs.

I had no name for my own reaction to the turn events had taken. Now that the spotlight was on Dad, the Highlands faded into the background. Scotland – the location shoot for a hoax, a place of bogus mythologising, sham tartanry – had lost its appeal. What Dad and I had been doing together, just at the moment our intimacy had begun to feel authentic, now seemed trivial. The fakery we had helped Mr Routh and the television crew to create interposed itself between us. With my walk-on part in a TV spoof, I had been his unwitting accomplice. No less than the wretched readers of the Scottish edition of the *Daily Express*, I had been had.

We drove back to England via Edinburgh. On the road out of Galashiels Dad stopped the car and knocked on the door of a house set back inside its own walled garden. A white-haired old lady answered the door and we were invited in and given tea. She had obviously been expecting us. She called Dad William, which meant she belonged to an early period in his life. Her own name was Enid Horsburgh. This lady, who was Dad's age, with her enormous bosom and behind, her skirt and jacket made out of Harris Tweed, reminded me of the film actress Margaret Rutherford as Professor Hatton-Jones in *Passport to Pimlico*. She was, I supposed, the same Enid Ballantine as the one in the 1911 photograph in Dad's pink cake tin of a family picnic at which Dad, in a sailor suit even then, was eight or nine years old, she pretty in a white dress and black stockings with her dark hair long and thick. She belonged to the time before the Flood, before the *Titanic* and the British Empire had sunk without a trace.

Lady Horsburgh made a big fuss of me. She thought I was marvellous – or perhaps what was marvellous was that William Luke should have managed to pull off something as conventional as producing a son as ordinary as me.

'I'm glad things worked out for you in the end, William,' she said.

'They nearly didn't!'

'Oh, I felt sure they would.'

Since they couldn't speak much more plainly than this in front of me, they discussed Dad's family: his mother, who had recently died, and his sisters, who were alive and well in Edinburgh, where we had just been – my grandmother and my aunts – none of whom I had ever seen. Except for his sister Mary, Dad's relations with his family had been difficult. The sinister Mr Watt and Miss Blacker had been the cause of the rift. I had never met any member of his family, his legal wife or his other offspring. Somewhere in the world Dad had sons my mother's age.

'I thought Enid was a poppet when I was a boy,' Dad said as the Alvis drove away from Enid's house and headed towards the English border. 'She was a lovely creature. The first girl I ever kissed. For a while I was quite gone on her – and she thought the world of me. She was the kind of nice girl Mother thought I should marry. How different my life would have been if I had!'

'Why didn't you?' I asked him.

Dad, baring his false teeth, grinned.

'Bloody-mindedness!'

When we got back to London a letter was waiting for me on the mantelpiece in my room. I recognised the pale green paper envelope and the loopy handwriting. I recognised the cheap Woolworth's perfume.

> My Darling
> Where are you? I have been so worried about you.
> I asked Julian and Dick but they didn't know any more than I did.
> I must talk to you! I know I have treated you cruelly but try to understand it from my point of view. Although you want less than Adam or any of those boys, in another way you want so much more. It frightens me how much you want. I'm too young for that. Please don't blame me if I behave badly. I can't help it.
> Talk to me! Oh dear. I'm going to cry!
>
> xxxx Charley

The Final Reckoning

The second to last time I saw Dad we tacked slowly up the steep lane that led from his home to the gate of the old churchyard on our way to the Eight Bells public house. Since his cornea operation five years earlier Dad had been forced to slow down. The strider had had to learn to shuffle, to move his feet forward without bending knee or ankle. He had begun to walk like an old man. He was eighty-two. He breathed rapidly through his mouth in order to maximise the volume of oxygen his lungs inhaled, puffing noisily to retard its exhalation. We tacked because the greater distance the manoeuvre involved was compensated for by the reduction in effort required to climb the lesser gradient. Walking at an angle to the incline of the hill reduced its steepness. It was, he claimed, a primitive low gear.

But the fifteenth-century lane that ran alongside the sheer eighteenth-century brick wall of the fourteenth-century churchyard eventually connected the Hampshire market town to the twentieth-century motorway. Vehicles occasionally cruised down the lane at a cool 20 mph, whereas our own zig-zag journey was being undertaken at hedgehog speed. Only after we had gained the crown of the road and we were in a position to see round the blind corner would we know if we had time to reach a decision whether to proceed onwards and upwards – or not. I was nervous but Dad, who had owned numerous fast motor cars in his life – most recently an ancient scarlet Triumph Spitfire – was, as usual, breezily confident. He made walking at 0.5 miles per hour as hair-raising an experience as riding beside him in the Spitfire had been prior to his cornea operation.

The agile ectomorph who in his prime had rarely paused for laggards to keep pace with him – either crossing the Bayswater Road or in his explanations of how logarithms worked – was shrunken and frail, a shell of a man who leaned on my arm on one side and on a stick on the other. Nevertheless, he was wearing his polished ox-blood brogues and, incongruous but stylish, his Oxfam Crombie over his blazer. His silk scarf was in the colours of Blake Term at Dartmouth, where he had come second in the 1916 cross-country event.

As we approached the apex of the camber, the opposite bend in the S of the lane came into view. A white car was descending towards us, decelerating on its approach to the town centre. Dad raised his stick as if he were hailing a cab in Sussex Gardens. The driver of the car had no choice, if he didn't want to risk colliding with an octogenarian pedestrian, but to decelerate rather more rapidly than had been his intention. We crossed in front of the now-stationary Volvo estate and Dad raised his stick once more, in acknowledgement of the driver's kindness. The stricken look on the face of the man behind the wheel as he idled the engine of his car on the dangerous narrow bend exactly expressed my own feelings.

It was a relief to reach the gate, enter the churchyard, climb the little hill and sit down on a bench donated by a deceased parishioner. In front of us were lichened gravestones bearing the names of the Susannahs and Samuels who had married in this church, ancient horse chestnut trees with their splendid pink candles, and the even more ancient, even more splendid church with its graceful slate steeple, serene as a gull's wing. We sat for several moments without speaking, contemplating the scene, while Dad got his breath back. To Dad, engineer and atheist, the beauty of church steeples was an expression of how successfully the architect had solved the trigonometry involved in suspending heavy objects to an optimum height above the earth's surface: eight bells, in this case. The E tenor alone weighed eighteen hundredweight. God, in his view, was a name for the coefficient in all things, a tricky equation whose solution would be arrived at sooner or later – in my lifetime, if not his.

'I'm sorry I can't give you any money,' he said after he had got his breath back. 'If I had any, I would . . .' *Puff. Puff.* '. . . You know that.'

Of course I knew that.

Today was Sunday. On Wednesday I would be crossing the George Washington Bridge, heading for the New Jersey Turnpike, Highway 81 and the Great Smoky Mountains. I planned to make my way across America, to travel overland in a driveaway car from New York to San Francisco by way of New Orleans, El Paso, Tucson. I thought I might drop in on my sister, who lived with her husband and son in a house with a garden in a suburb of Houston. I was interested to find out whether or not, somewhere over the rainbow where skies are blue, the dreams she had dared to dream had come true. But I wasn't going to need Dad's money. I had received a £5,000 advance from the London publisher Hamish Hamilton to complete a book of fiction set in various bars of America.

'Did you know I managed a speakeasy for a short time in New York? Nineteen twenty-five. No, 'twenty-six . . .'

Of course I knew.

After a moment, he asked me whether I was still interested in the dusty unopened bottle of twelve-year-old single malt whisky that stood in its cardboard box on the bookcase in his bedroom – twenty-two years, if you counted the decade it had stood there, gathering dust. I assured him I was. When hadn't I been?

'You know what you have to do, don't you . . . ?'

Of course I knew what I had to do.

'. . . It won't be long now.'

He wanted me to leave but he didn't want me to be away.

I said nothing. We were at the end of June. I didn't plan to be back until January the following year. Plenty of time remained.

We stood up, Dad holding on to my arm with his free hand. As we continued the descent down the other side of the graveyard, the curate was striding up the path towards us.

'You've missed the service, Fergie, I'm afraid,' he called. 'It finished half an hour ago!'

Dad bared his too-white false teeth in delight at the curate's leg-pulling.

'Well, we're not too late for the Eight Bells, Donald!' he quipped as soon as we were level. 'Why don't you join us?'

Because it was Sunday and this was obviously out of the question, Donald laughed. Dad introduced me to the young curate and we shook hands.

'Your father is trying to persuade me that Jesus of Nazareth was an early socialist,' he said, grinning at the idea. 'A sort of anti-Pharisee labour organiser.'

As if this was something I didn't know. Dad's notions about Life, Death, Evolution, History, the Cosmos, God, Jesus of Nazareth, had been shaped by those of lower-middle-class H. G. Wells and the aristo-Communist scientist J. B. S.

Haldane. Shaw, Russell, Huxley. Atheist anti-Establishment thinkers.

Like Dad, Donald was ex-RN and had been a rugby player. They had much in common, including an interest in scripture. Donald said he had nearly finished the book Dad had lent him. They must get together one evening to discuss it over a pint. The book – I hardly needed to be told – was called *The Nazarene Gospel Restored*, a scholarly work by Robert Graves, whose purpose in writing it had been to examine the historical basis for the facts of the Gospels. It had been the family Bible in our house throughout my childhood. I had read it when I was sixteen. For a man without faith, Dad was an expert in talking about it. He had always enjoyed the company of clergymen, with whom he was courteously disputatious. Clergymen, for their part, humoured him, touched by the vigour with which he sought to provoke in them, through the application of Occam's razor, a crisis of faith.

With a cheery wave, Donald hurried towards the church, late for something.

Dad and I covered the descending gradient between the lower gate of the churchyard and the door of the Eight Bells without incident. All the same, by the time we reached our destination, I needed a drink.

Dad sat down at the bar on the stool reserved for him while the landlord, without being asked, reached up for his mug, a half-pint pewter grain measure, from its hook above the Badgers Ales pump. He pulled Dad's beer.

'David, this is my son,' Dad said.

David pulled my pint.

'He's very popular, your dad,' he said. 'Has us in stitches. And you can probably imagine, his ideas aren't what you would call fashionable in these parts.'

Socialism. Atheism. String theory . . .

'Everyone pulls his leg when he lays into Margaret Thatcher. Don't worry, it's all done friendly. He gives as good as he gets. We love him.'

I was delighted to hear this, but it didn't sound like my dad, who had possessed a talent, ever since I had known him, for rubbing people up the wrong way, especially people in pubs.

'He's done a lot of things in his life, your father has,' David said.

Except for ourselves the pub was empty. Dad had insisted we set off early in order to be at the bar before the Sunday snacks disappeared. When David's wife Linda arrived with trays of delicacies, she laid before Dad his own personal consignment: shelled prawns, white crab meat on Carr's water biscuits, smoked mussels. Dad, having discreetly removed his teeth with his pocket handkerchief, scanned the selection.

'What, Linda? *No olives?*'

'Oh, I'm sorry, Fergie. David! . . .' Linda called over her shoulder. '. . . Will you bring a bowl of those pitted Kalamata olives Fergie likes.'

The pub filled up. We drank and talked with Dad's chums, several of whom pressed me into accepting a half pint of bitter. He told the story of how the two-seater aircraft he was in had been shot down in Anatolia by Kemal Atatürk's militiamen in 1920 – the short version.

To enter the United States I had applied for a new passport and to do that I had needed to produce a birth certificate. Examining this document carefully for the first time, I saw that who it said I was did not exactly coincide with whom I purported to be.

My father's name on my birth certificate was a false one –

and so, for that matter, was my mother's. For 'William Luke' he had substituted 'William Duncan' and for 'Ferguson' he had substituted 'Grant'. My mother, no doubt under his influence, had substituted Grant for her own name, which was Haworth, to imply that she was married to the father of her children. The trusting Registrar of Births, Marriages and Deaths in the Town Hall in sleepy Tunbridge Wells, Mr Frederick Stridworthy, seems to have taken my parents' false declarations of who they were at face value. The threat of prosecution for making a false statement had not deterred Dad. But it followed that my own legal name was also false. My true name didn't appear on my own birth certificate. Already, only a few days old, I had become entangled in my dad's rearrangement of what is legal and what is true.

Dad's doctoring of his identity had been only in part to enable him to fly kites, throw creditors, the taxman and Ministry of Labour employees, off his scent. Although he enjoyed frustrating representatives of the state – because he found it irksome to accept any jurisdiction over himself – the main reason he assumed different names was because it allowed him to step away from the person his family had intended him to be. Luke Scotland, Bill Grant, W. L. Ferguson were versions of himself he had tried out. In 1939, while he was working as a design engineer for the Wireless & Telephone Company in Liverpool as Bill Grant, he had taken a shine to a pretty seventeen-year-old girl who worked in the office, who liked him to take her to the cinema to see Groucho Marx films. He had taken her to an ILP meeting at which, she said, a man called George Orwell had spoken.

I zig-zagged across the United States from New York to San Francisco in driveaway cars, my route determined by the

destinations of the cars to be delivered. Lynchburg, Virginia. Texarkana. Silver City, New Mexico. Tucson, Arizona. In downtown bars I allowed myself to be drawn into conversation with strangers and waited for events to unfold. Later, in cheap hotels, I turned these encounters into fiction on my 1935 Remington portable typewriter.

The last time I saw Dad he was lying in a coma in an NHS bed in Basingstoke General Hospital. The modern single ward, a corner room with windows in two walls, was bathed in a dusty-blue winter sunlight. If you removed the adrenalin drip and the oxygen apparatus and the student nurse you could have been in a three-star airport hotel anywhere in the world. It was clean, secular, functional, an appropriate place for the atheist engineer to make his final empirical observation. Dad had always enjoyed air travel and, in his impatience to be somewhere else, inclined to eschew valediction.

I had arrived back from the United States the day before, my book almost finished, just as Dad's pleurisy was developing into pneumonia, in time for him to be informed of my safe return. Too late for me to tell him that my sister had indeed found in Houston the thing she had always wanted: a loving family. Almost immediately he had lost consciousness, as if the news of my homecoming had given him permission to relax his hold on life. My mum and I and Sarah sat on the edge of his bed, drinking Scotch as the sun set over the hospital car park.

As soon as I saw that they were giving him adrenalin I knew the game was up. It had never been a substance he had ever had much difficulty manufacturing for himself – or in other people. He took corners fast, using his gears in preference to his brakes. Only a half a dozen years earlier, at the age of seventy-six, he had driven to Town in order to entertain some fellow who had expressed an interest in one of his projects. Leaving the restaurant – nothing concluded – the better for half a bottle of claret, Dad had roared into the westbound lane of traffic in his ageing scarlet Triumph Spitfire. A passing foot-patrol constable, observing the driver's reluctance to indicate his intentions, attempted to arrest the car's progress. Dad – according to the constable's testimony in court – had put his foot down. The constable had commandeered a passing cab and given chase, halted the sports car at some traffic lights, dragged out the ancient tearaway, breathalysed and nicked him. It had been this, losing his licence, not being able to run around Town in motor cars any more, as much as his cornea operation, that had done for Dad. Once the adrenalin had ceased to flow, it was only a matter of time.

I was grateful that it was not the death he had schooled us to be ready for, something not to be taken lying down but on the chin. There was no flat-footed copper here for him to outwit, Dad's deeds in his book, only an angelic teenage nurse, unconcerned what sins he had committed, who lifted the oxygen mask whenever his breathing became irregular.

Dad's cremation took place in a red-brick mausoleum on the outskirts of Aldershot on a very cold, very sunny February morning. The briers, thriving on phosphorous and other trace elements, had been cut back hard. Sarah and I, having arrived by cab early, took the opportunity to warm ourselves up in the empty vestibule. We swayed against each other to a 78 rpm recording of Fred Astaire singing through the tiny speakers of my Sony cassette player:

> *There may be trouble ahead.*
> *There may be teardrops to shed.*
> *Before they ask us to pay the bill*
> *And while we still*
> *Have the chance,*
> *Let's face the music and dance.*

Sarah had been fond of Dad, who had flirted with her shamelessly. We danced until a Daimler arrived with my mother and my brother and his family. We exchanged brittle greetings in the frosty atmosphere.

It was a fucking miserable occasion. No friends had been invited – or even informed. There were no ne'er-do-well pub chums to enliven the gathering. Only members of the immediate family were present – five adults, three children – and these all had ambivalent feelings about the deceased. My sister had sent flowers from Texas. Except for the fact that my mother wept, the ceremony was without ritual, music, meaning or humour. During the fifteen minutes it took the coffin to slide out of view I listened through the earpiece of my Sony to my dad's verbatim account of how the aeroplane he was in had been shot down during the Greaco-Turkish War by Kemal Atatürk's irregular militia – the full version:

> '. . . The old Caliphate government was held captive by the Allies in Constant. Atatürk simply proclaimed a new government in Ankara. I was in HMS Centurion – one of your old Iron Duke type battleships – KG5 Class. We were guard ship up in the Gulf of Izmir – Smyrna, then, of course . . .'
>
> 'When would this be?'
>
> This would be in August 1920. Atatürk was kicking the Greeks out of Anatolia. It was a bloody awful business. British policy was to support the Greeks. Centurion's guns were bombarding the Turkish positions. The terrain there is a series of foothills that rise to higher and higher hills and the Turks had their troops just over the crest of these hills. The result was we couldn't use our guns at all. We either fired on our own troops or over where there weren't any troops at all . . .'
>
> 'Were you firing from the bay below?'
>
> 'Yes, that's right.'
>
> 'Why couldn't you howitzer them?'
>
> 'We had no howitzers in the Navy. Our guns were meant to fire so that they landed at a 30-degree angle, almost in a flat trajectory. Close inshore, to be accurate to fire, they simply went into the side of the hills. There was no way of hitting the enemy.
>
> 'The gunners had learnt this so they decided to use 13.5 shrapnel which, you can imagine, is a devastating weapon, full of tiny little 13.5 steel balls. Before they could use it, they needed to know where the trenches were along the ridge of hills. The coastal villages – where these Turkish militiamen had their wives – had been taken by the Gordon Highlanders. These militiamen were local patriots, you know what I mean? They weren't

regulars. They believed in Kemal Atatürk, who was trying to drag Turkey into the twentieth century.

'But the Turks knew how to fight. It had only been four years before that their regulars had given our troops a bloody nose at Gallipoli.

'Well, the gunners wanted a drawing of their position so, because I could draw, they sent me up in a de Havilland 9A to make one. I went up first with an RAF type to have a look-see. I hadn't anything with me to make a sketch. I had just to make a reconnaissance, to see if it was feasible. That went off all right. It was my first trip in an aeroplane, as a matter of fact, and I thought it was great fun – but, coming down, the silly sod landed the wrong side of the flat strip they were using as an airfield. He put his undercarriage – they had fixed undercarriages, you understand – straight into a ditch. It went over on its nose and I caught the gun rack on my jaw, smashed my jaw and knocked two teeth out.

'Well, they sent me up the next day. I'd another officer, another DH9A, and this time a pad with sketches I had drawn from the chart of where these mountain tops would lie. We flew about forty feet above the trenches so that I could get a really good look at them. We saw that we were being fired at but we didn't think anything of it. Half these chaps had nothing but muzzle-loaders full of stones, pellets, any rubbish they could stuff down them, and they had been firing this at us. When they did have weapons, they were excellent German ones. Turning round for our final run, our engine failed. No petrol. The DH9A had a special tank in the mid-section of the upper wing, you see, and it had been peppered. Dead engine. No petrol at all!

'With the valley behind us, no way of getting over the top and home, the pilot had to bring her down. We landed in a rough bit of flattish ground and bumped to a stop. The pilot was in khaki and I was in full midshipman's whites. I had no pistol on because I had found, the first time I went up, the bloody thing got in the way, a big Webley in a holster in the cockpit. But it was an order. You weren't allowed ashore without a gun and I hadn't got mine with me. All I had was the deck watch and my pad full of these sketches. The pilot – would you believe it? – climbed out and scarpered! Just disappeared. Left me on my own. I ran after him and then thought better of it. I returned to the aircraft. I had to climb up and put my head down into the canopy to pick up my papers and in doing so the deck watch fell out of my pocket. I don't know if you know but a deck watch is a very delicate chronometer. There was no way it would work again after falling down three or four feet. So I just left it there. I collected my pad and got out and proceeded to walk across the dip in the hills.

'It was getting latish. I headed up the escarpment. I daren't look back. I just went solemnly up the hill thinking I'd probably get a bullet between my shoulder blades sooner or later.

'But I did know that there had been an arrangement which was the laughing stock of the whole British Expeditionary Force in the Gulf of Izmir. The Turks who lived in the villages with their families had an informal arrangement with the brigadier of the 18th Hussars, who was senior officer. At the end of hostilities, when the sun touched the hill, they would be allowed back into their villages. Before the sun rose, they had to be out of them. In exchange our troops had arak and food . . .

'I must have been about half a mile from the top of the hill when I heard a whole lot of laughter behind me. I turned round – frightened out of my wits! – and there were all these Turkish militiamen laughing and waving and pointing at the sun, which was just about to touch the crest of the horizon. It must have been that much off it, but as far as they were concerned it was sunset and they followed me in. They were within twenty or thirty yards of me when we came to Jenicoy – that was the name of this village. A captain came out to meet me.

'"Snotty," he said. "Are these your prisoners?"

'"Good Lord no, sir. I'm theirs. They just pointed to the sun and said, 'War over.'"

'"Oh," he said. "That shower. All right. You had better report to your officer. Where's your pilot?"

'I said: "He just scarpered. Ran off."

'He must have been shot. No one ever heard of him again, as far as I could make out. But running off into the bush in khaki like that, he would have been shot out of hand by the Turks, if they caught him.

'Anyway, the two-striper on watch duty sent a signal by heliograph to the bridge of *Centurion*: "Midshipman returned. Please send picket boat to collect." I went down to the water's edge – we had a tiny quay, just a few stones on the beach. Picket boat came in. I was taken on board. I arrived on deck looking filthy, of course – sweaty and dirty. No pistol, but with my clutch of papers. There was a sub-lieutenant to meet me. He said, "The commander wants to see you in his cabin." He took me down there, knocked on the door. Had me in. The commander looked me up and down and said, "What the hell have you been doing?"

'I said, "We got shot down and the pilot scarpered. I went back for the reconnaissance drawings. I think you'll find them accurate. We did several runs. I've marked where the trenches are. The Turks fired at us and must have holed us –"

'"Never mind that now. Why are you not wearing a pistol?"

'So I told him.

'"I found when I made the dummy run yesterday that I couldn't move in the cockpit with a holster on so I left it on board."

> 'He said: "What about the deck watch?"
>
> 'I said I had lost that.
>
> 'He said: "That's on your slops-chit. You should have been more careful. It should have been hitched to your uniform. For breaking regulations and going ashore without your revolver and losing the ship's deck watch . . ." He turned round to the sub-lieutenant and said, "Give him six on the arse."
>
> 'The sub took me down to the bathroom and gave me six on the arse. That was all I got out of it.'

After the ceremony, my mum and my brother's family returned home in the Daimler. Sarah and I followed in a taxi. But as the cab approached the market town where we were to reassemble my courage failed and when the ancient church spire came into view, serene on top of the hill, I succumbed to the impulse to stop the cab, jump out and run into the nearest public house. Sarah continued on in the cab to explain to the family that I would be delayed. They would understand. I was, after all, the youngest one. His father's son. Someone who could not be relied on.

It wasn't yet midday and the pub I chose was empty. At the bar I bade the landlord good morning and ordered a half pint of Badger's. David didn't recognise me from my brief visit five months before. As far as he was concerned, I was what victuallers call 'passing trade'.

'In my father's mug, please, David,' I said. 'If that's all right.'

I nodded up towards the polished pewter grain measure hanging on its hook over the pumps. David hesitated.

'I'm Fergie's son. We met in June. You probably don't remember me.'

David didn't remember me but at least I was no longer passing trade. I allowed him to remain cheerful for as long as it took him to draw my half pint and enquire after my dad's health. I emptied the mug before I gave him the juice.

'Dad died on Tuesday. I've just come from his funeral.'

David blinked. He opened his mouth and appropriate words came out but I could tell he had gone onto automatic pilot. He was shocked, upset, hurt. I felt sorry for him. It was a moving experience to watch my piece of information enter the consciousness of a near-stranger. His dismay conducted to earth my own grief. The electrical current flowing through a body, Dad had frequently pointed out, is equal to the strength of the current divided by the resistance of the body.

'But he was only in here a week or so ago! Sitting where you're sitting.'

'It was all very sudden, mercifully. Shingles, pleurisy, pneumonia. You know Dad. He was never one to hang around.'

David took my dad's empty mug out of my hand, filled it from the pump and handed it back to me. He pulled a half for himself.

'Here's to Fergie,' he said. 'He was a one-off.'

We raised our mugs and drank to the memory of Fergie, my dad. This simple act of fellowship in a public house with a man I hardly knew provided the human comment the death of a person requires, something the unceremonious disposal of the body in Aldershot had failed to do.

'*Arsy-versy*, that was one of his Navy expressions, wasn't it? Now everyone who comes into the pub uses it. Everything is *arsy-versy*. Fergie had us in stitches.'

As the pub filled up and customers approached the bar to buy drinks and exchange greetings, David – or another – murmured to the new arrival: 'Did you know? Fergie has died. That's his son over here.' One after the other they came across, shook my hand, said how much they were going to miss the old boy, asked me to pass on their condolences to my mother, and filled the pewter grain measure with beer. One expressed regret that he had not been given the opportunity to attend the cremation service. Another suggested the pub hold a charity night in Fergie's honour, recalling the Beaujolais Nouveau Night at which he had turned up in a beret with a string of onions and had refused to speak English to anyone. To me it seemed extraordinarily benign of Providence to have allowed the Old Man to end his days in the company of such a warm-hearted group of chums who had no idea what a difficult bugger he had been in his prime.

When it was time for me to go, Linda asked me if I should like to hang on to Dad's half-pint grain measure. I would have liked to. I possessed nothing of his. What would I do with half a dozen disassembled Japanese radio cassette recorders, his collection of India rubbers, F-lead pencils, matchboxes containing electrical terminals, his battered 1940 edition of *Maths for the Million*?

'I'd like David to keep it,' I told her.

David was pleased to accept Dad's measure and we shook hands. I left the pub, thankful that for once in my life I had done the right thing.

Taking the short-cut across the church burial ground, I sat down for few a moments on the bench where Dad and I had rested on the last occasion I had been here. Everything was almost the same. Under the lichened headstones the Samuels and Susannahs were still waiting for Judgement Day. The branches of the horse chestnut trees were bare. Alongside me in the cold sunlight was the space Dad had occupied when we were last here. It was hard to believe that this empty space would always be there, wherever I went in life.

My heart was light, my step high, when I entered my

brother's house, perhaps too light and too high. I came in on the wrong note, grinning at the long faces. I glanced at Sarah, who signalled to me telepathically that I was in the doghouse. I was late. Lunch – *luncheon*, Dad preferred to call it – was awaiting my arrival to be served. I could see how angry with me my brother was by his determination not to show it. The head prefect was giving me a lesson in self-control.

We sat down to a meal of cold supermarket ham and baked potatoes. The atmosphere was tense. I did what Dad would have done in the circumstances, pretended not to notice the atmosphere nor anybody's discomfiture. I may have been a teeny bit drunk. I didn't give a damn about anybody's discomfiture. I was hearty and cracked a few jokes. I related the events that had taken place over in the Eight Bells: Dad's chums had been sorry to hear of his death, had sent messages of condolence to Mum and wanted to know if she would have any objections to them organising a charity Fergie Night to mark his passing. I had given Dad's grain measure to the landlord . . .

'You had no right to do that.'

My brother had spoken.

The temperature rose over the cold cuts. The well-mannered children, reading the situation – or, perhaps, obeying a parental cue I missed – made their escape. Lucky things.

I said: 'Dad had a lot of friends in the pub. He was very popular. He had them in stitches.'

'I know.'

'You *know*? If you *knew*, why didn't you invite them to his funeral?'

'It wasn't any of their business.'

'Of course it was their business! They had a right to be told about the funeral arrangements.'

'Who says they do? *You?* You don't know anything about them!'

'And you *do*?'

'I know who they are.'

'It doesn't matter who they are. They were Dad's friends. They should have been there.'

'Mum wanted a quiet family funeral. She didn't want a crowd of pub hangers-on.'

'What you mean is, *you* wanted a quiet family funeral. *You* didn't want a crowd of pub hangers-on.'

What he meant was, if the ne'er-do-wells from the Eight Bells had attended the funeral they would have had to have been invited back for a drink afterwards.

Mum, while her sons bickered, wept into her hankie.

In my brother's view, my sloping off to the pub, announcing Dad's death to all and sundry, giving away his pewter grain measure to a pub landlord, had been thoughtless and self-indulgent. It was behaviour – he didn't need to say it; we all knew what he meant – *typical of Dad.*

My brother – head teacher, local councillor, pillar of the community – had consciously fashioned himself into a mirror-image of his father. Determined to be the opposite of him in every respect, he had rejected his dad's restless, reckless delinquency. An apostle of the blameless life, he himself had never done anything thoughtless or self-indulgent, reckless or delinquent. He was cautious, dutiful, sensible, possessor of those very virtues his father had been especially contemptuous of. While genial to one another in their everyday dealings, each in his heart had despised the other. The one respectable, the other disreputable, both had been anathema to the other. Like the clear and opaque elements in a photographic negative, each was what the other was not. And there wasn't anything either of them could do about it.

It was obvious to me why Dad – who had spent the last half decade of his life as my brother's next-door neighbour – had found a refuge in the jolly atmosphere of the Eight Bells where he didn't have to mind his Ps and Qs. The pub had provided him with the opportunity to reinvent himself yet again, a new captive audience for his stories about his life and times. It was the stage for what he knew would be positively his final performance.

The following summer Sarah and I cycled from the house of her cousin Gerald in Newcastle upon Tyne to that of our friend Gordon in Tweedbank, Peeblesshire. It was a distance of about eighty-five miles that took us two days to cover. The Cheviot hills lay between the two map references; it often drizzled hard. Even though we were riding bespoke touring bikes that had Reynolds 531 double-butted frames with lugless drop-outs, hand-built alloy wheels and Brooks B17 leather saddles, the hills were arduous. They were even more arduous for me when you took into account the extra weight I was carrying in my panniers. In the right an unopened twenty-three-year-old bottle of Glenlivet single malt whisky, still in its dusty box with the original price label: £6.77. In the left Dad, a funeral parlour plastic urn containing his ashes.

By happy happenstance Gordon's home town on the Tweed lay a dozen miles from where my father had been born. The first sunny morning after we arrived the three of us cycled along the disused railway line that followed the meandering course of the river upstream, past Caddonfoot – Caddon was on my birth certificate – through Traquair Forest, until we reached our destination on the OS map: a stretch of the Tweed opposite Pirn Crag – Pirn was on my sister's birth certificate. We dismounted and wheeled our bikes over the sward to the river's edge where a pair of dippers was stalking. We set out our picnic in a sunny spot. The Tweed at this point was shallow, fast-moving, clear; the sunlit shale bed of the river visible through the onrushing water. Above its quiet roar we could hear the distant clamour of children playing. Hidden behind ancient cedar trees on the opposite bank, a rural comprehensive school stood on the site of The Pirn, the long-demolished big house between Walkerburn and Traquair, where the family of the Reverend John Ferguson of St Andrews, the Episcopalian kirk in Innerleithen, had lived through the last years of Queen Victoria's reign to the end of the Great War. There, on 18 October 1902, St Luke' Day, William Luke had come into the world. He had been baptised and christened by his own father at the font of his father's church. Among these hills, along this stretch of water, he had run wild, flown kites, fished trout, been happy. Here, at least, he had been innocent.

After the deaths of Duncan and Ian in France, Dad acted as if no ties of duty existed between him and any person or institution. Responsibility for the slaughter of his brothers he placed on the shoulders of members of the established order: the Church, the state, the property-owning caste to which his family had belonged and whose values it had shared. He had left the Navy in 1921 because he hated it, because he hated taking orders. He was disinclined to submit to any form of authority over himself; all rules, even necessary, conventional regulations such as the Highway Code, he tended to disregard. There had been periods in his life during which the needle of his moral compass had departed from true north. Temperamentally, he liked to sail close to the wind, as close as he could get to the eye of the storm. Of his six children with three women, only one had been born in wedlock. Only his patrician distain for lower-middle-class values had shielded us and our mother from obloquy. He didn't give two hoots what rules the readers of the *Daily Mail* and the *Express* thought he had transgressed. The only rules he respected, and which in the end gave his life coherence, were those of mathematics: the slide-rule, the book of logarithms, calculus. The marvellous neatness and beauty of his mechanical drawings were in contrast to the mess he had made of his life.

Remarkably and against all the odds, in the final reckoning on the double-entry balance sheet of what was owed and what owing, Dad's assets had not ended up in the red column. The closing statement of his account at his branch of the Midland Bank had been in credit to the sum of £13.38, sufficient for his widow to purchase a new set of cotton bed linen in the sale at Alders in Aldershot.

At the water's edge I removed my Italian cycling shoes, then my socks. I broke the seal on the cap of the malt and handed the green triangular bottle to Gordon, took the plastic urn from Sarah and opened that also – the three of us involuntarily inhaling the puff of white dust that issued forth. I took the bottle back from Gordon and poured a generous dram into the urn, libating the contents. Sarah held out three empty glasses. After I had half-filled each of them, returned the bottle to Gordon, accepted one of the glasses myself, the three of us raised our whisky to the life of the man who had given me mine. After so many years, so many adventures, misadventures and close shaves in so many corners of the world, he was back where he had set out from: home. The circle – with satisfying geometrical symmetry – was complete.

Opposite the cedar trees screening the comprehensive school I waded barefoot into the Tweed until the rapid, ice-cold, crag-cleansed, sky-reflecting water eddied over my toes, between my legs and around my knees – and onto this current I scattered Dad's remains. A fine cloud like cigar smoke drifted upwards, as if to acknowledge that the soul of the man himself had always tended more towards the aerial than to the aquatic. The heavier, grittier pieces sank through the flow to the riverbed. The lighter fragments were swiftly carried downstream on the surface of the water in the direction of the pair of dippers, Coldstream, Berwick and the North Sea.